ARCHITECTURE
INSPIRATIONS

ÉDITIONS
PLACE DES
VICTOIRES

© 2009, Éditions Place des Victoires
6, rue du Mail - 75002 Paris,
pour la présente édition.
www.victoires.com

ISBN : 978-2-8099-0072-9
Dépôt légal : 4ᵉ trimestre 2009
Imprimé en Chine

Projet éditorial :
© 2009 **LOFT Publications**
Via Laietana, 32, 4º, Of. 92
08003 Barcelone, Espagne
Tél. : +34 932 688 088
Fax : +34 932 687 073
loft@loftpublications.com
www.loftpublications.com

Coordination éditoriale :
Simone K. Schleifer

Assistante :
Aitana Lleonart

Éditrice :
Cristina Paredes Benítez

Direction artistique :
Feyyaz (mail@feyyaz.com)

Mise en page :
Cristina Granero Navarro, Nil Solà Serra

Coordination des traductions :
Équipe éditoriale, Barcelone

Traductions :
Jane Wintle (anglais), Michael Ficerai (français), Donatella Talpo (italien), Susanne Engler (espagnol)

LOFT possède les droits de reproduction des images présentées dans cet ouvrage. LOFT a respecté les droits d'auteur. LOFT garantit que cet ouvrage ne contient aucune image obscène ou irrespectueuse.

Toutes les démarches nécessaires ont été faites afin d'identifier et de contacter les détenteurs de copyrights et leurs ayants droit. Toute erreur ou omission sera corrigée en cas de réimpression.

Tous droits réservés. Il est rigoureusement interdit, sans le consentement des titulaires du copyright ou de leurs ayants droit, sous peine des sanctions prévues par la loi en vigueur, toute reproduction intégrale ou partielle de cet ouvrage par un quelconque mode ou procédé, tels que la photocopie, le traitement de texte, ainsi que la distribution de l'ouvrage sous forme de location ou de prêt public.

INTRODUCTION	4
MAISONS DE VILLE	10
MAISONS DE MONTAGNE	140
MAISONS DE VILLAGE	216
MAISONS DE CAMPAGNE	392
PAVILLONS DE BANLIEUE	470
MAISONS SUR LA CÔTE	588
CRÉDITS	704

Contemporary residential architecture is a clear reflection of social and economic change. Leaving aside the familiar terraced homes found on so many housing estates, this architectural field is producing novel, innovative designs showing technical advances in construction technology applied to single family homes. This book offers a comprehensive selection of family residences from all over the world, original, personalised constructions which reflect their owners' requisites and preferences. New family models and a greater degree of occupational mobility are just two of the many factors currently redefining the home. Owners today have access to more information, are far more knowledgeable of architecture and interior design, and have a much better defined idea of their requirements. Hence, projects are built to meet specific demands and solutions are devised individually for each client. We find instances where huge windows break down the barrier between indoors and outdoors, flooding the home with natural light; where ample multiple-function spaces or rooms are fully customised for specific uses; where studies and work areas are clearly distinguished from living and resting areas, and where bedrooms have become a secluded, intimate part of the house. In today's home, anything is possible.

The residences reviewed in this volume show how a very wide range of materials can be used to adapt constructions to their surroundings, and not vice-versa. In most cases, these materials are highly compatible with nature and the environment. The architectural programme in conjunction with geographical location are instrumental in defining a house's exterior forms. The following pages portray original solutions and novel techniques for blending architecture with its entourage or conversely creating a powerful visual and aesthetic contrast. All options are possible: there are no limits to interior designers' and architects' creativity. Each of the homes in "Architecture Inspirations" are comprehensive projects where exterior and interior design carry equal weight. This book aims to present the latest trends in residential architecture and interior design, propose a variety of styles, and serve as a source of inspiration to readers. Furthermore, this collection may suggest ideas for building a new house or for redecorating the home, with practical, ingenious, audacious schemes for creating personalised environs and homes fully adapted to individual lifestyles. It is organised in chapters where projects are grouped by geographical location (city and suburban, village, country, mountain or waterfront) for maximum clarity and so that readers may identify instantly with the works illustrated.

Die heutige Wohnhausarchitektur spiegelt die gesellschaftlichen und wirtschaftlichen Veränderungen in unserer Gesellschaft wider. Wenn man von den hinlänglich bekannten Reihenhäusern in bestimmten Siedlungsgebieten absieht, hat die Architektur in diesem Sektor ebenfalls neue und innovative Gebäude hervorgebracht, an denen man erkennen kann, wie die Technik und die Fortschritte auch bei der Errichtung von Einfamilienhäusern angewandt werden. Dieses Buch stellt eine umfassende Auswahl an Häusern auf der ganzen Welt zusammen, sehr persönlich gestaltete und originelle Gebäude, die die Anforderungen und den Geschmack der Eigentümer erkennen lassen. Die neuen Familienmodelle und die größere Mobilität innerhalb der Bevölkerung aus beruflichen Gründen sind nur zwei der Gründe, die die heutigen Anforderungen an ein Wohnhaus definieren. Heutzutage sind die Hauseigentümer besser informiert, sie besitzen gewisse Kenntnisse der Architektur und der Innenarchitektur und wissen genau, was sie wollen. Die Häuser werden so gebaut, dass sie ganz bestimmten Anforderungen genügen und es werden konkrete Lösungen für jeden Kunden gesucht. So gibt es häufig große Fenster, die sich nach außen öffnen und reichlich Tageslicht ins Innere lassen, weite Räume, die mehreren Funktionen dienen und Zimmer, die ganz konkret für eine bestimmte Nutzung entworfen wurden. Die Ateliers und Arbeitsräume unterscheiden sich ganz deutlich von den Räumen, die der Ruhe und Freizeit dienen, und die Schlafzimmer sind die privatesten und zurückgezogensten Räume in diesen Häusern. In der Wohnung der heutigen Zeit findet alles seinen Platz.

Die Häuser, die in diesem Buch vorgestellt werden, sind aus sehr verschiedenartigen Materialien konstruiert, die sich an die Umgebung anpassen und nicht umgekehrt. Die meisten dieser Gebäude behandeln die umgebende Natur mit großem Respekt. Sowohl die räumlichen Anforderungen der Familien als auch die geographische Lage trugen zur Definition der äußeren Form des jeweiligen Hauses bei. Auf diesen Seiten werden originelle Lösungen und neue Techniken vorgestellt, die entweder die Architektur in ihre Umgebung integrieren oder einen großen visuellen und ästhetischen Kontrast schaffen. Alle Optionen sind möglich und es gibt keine Grenzen für die Arbeit der Architekten und Innenarchitekten. Die Häuser in Architektur Inspirationen sind integrale Projekte, sowohl was die Linien der Gebäude als auch die Innengestaltung betrifft, beides hat den gleichen Stellenwert. Ziel dieses Buches ist es, die neusten Trends im Bereich der Wohnhausarchitektur und Innenarchitektur zu zeigen, verschiedene Stile vorzuschlagen und als Inspirationsquelle zu dienen. Außerdem kann diese Auswahl an Gestaltungsmöglichkeiten sowohl Ideen zur Errichtung eines Neubaus als auch zur Umgestaltung bereits existierender Räumlichkeiten geben. Praktische, einfallsreiche und gewagte Lösungen schaffen eine besondere Atmosphäre und die Häuser passen sich an den Lebensrhythmus des Einzelnen an. Die Häuser werden in verschiedenen Kapiteln vorgestellt, wobei sie nach ihrer geographischen Lage wie Stadt und Stadtrand, kleine Dörfer, Land, Gebirge oder am Wasser geordnet sind, um sie so dem Leser näher zu bringen.

La arquitectura residencial contemporánea es un claro reflejo de los cambios sociales y económicos de la sociedad. Dejando de lado las consabidas casas adosadas de algunas urbanizaciones, en este campo de la arquitectura se desarrollan también novedosas construcciones que permiten apreciar cómo se han adaptado las técnicas y los avances en la construcción a la creación de viviendas unifamiliares. Este libro presenta una amplia y cuidada selección de residencias de todo el mundo, construcciones personalizadas y originales que reflejan las necesidades y los gustos de sus propietarios. Los nuevos modelos de familia y una mayor movilidad laboral de la población, por poner sólo dos ejemplos, han redefinido las necesidades reales de una casa. Actualmente, los propietarios disponen de una información más amplia, poseen más conocimientos de arquitectura e interiorismo y saben lo que quieren con mayor exactitud. Así pues, los proyectos se construyen en función de requerimientos específicos y se diseñan soluciones concretas para cada cliente. Podemos encontrar, por ejemplo, grandes ventanales que abren los hogares al exterior e inundan de luz los interiores, amplios espacios con múltiples funciones y estancias perfectamente diseñadas para un uso específico. Los estudios o zonas de trabajo se pueden diferenciar claramente de las áreas de descanso y de ocio, y los dormitorios se convierten en los espacios más íntimos de la casa. La vivienda contemporánea se abre a todas las posibilidades.

Las residencias presentadas en este volumen muestran una gran diversidad de materiales que consiguen adaptar las construcciones al entorno, y no al revés. La mayoría de ellos son respetuosos con el medio ambiente y con la naturaleza. Las necesidades del programa arquitectónico, así como la ubicación geográfica, contribuyen a definir las formas exteriores de la vivienda. En estas páginas se muestran soluciones originales y técnicas novedosas que o bien integran la arquitectura en el entorno o bien crean un gran contraste visual y estético. Todas las opciones son posibles y no hay límite a las creaciones de los arquitectos e interioristas. *Architecture Inspirations* reúne proyectos integrales en los que tanto las líneas de la construcción como el diseño de los interiores son igualmente importantes. Este libro tiene como objetivo mostrar las últimas tendencias en arquitectura residencial e interiorismo, proponer diversos estilos y ser fuente de inspiración para los lectores. Además, esta selección puede sugerir ideas tanto para la construcción de una nueva casa como para la redecoración de los interiores de la residencia habitual. Soluciones prácticas, ingeniosas y atrevidas para crear atmósferas propias y viviendas que se adaptan al ritmo de vida de cada uno. La organización en capítulos agrupa los proyectos en función de su situación geográfica (ciudades y periferia, pequeñas poblaciones, campo, montaña y junto al agua) para acercarse al lector y para que éste pueda identificarse con las propuestas presentadas.

L'architecture résidentielle contemporaine est le reflet des évolutions socio-économiques de notre société. Faisons l'impasse sur les maisons mitoyennes en lotissements et concentrons-nous sur les maisons individuelles. On assiste au développement de constructions novatrices permettant d'apprécier l'évolution des techniques et les audaces architecturales. Cet ouvrage présente une ample sélection de maisons du monde entier, des constructions personnalisées et originales qui reflètent les besoins et les goûts de leurs propriétaires. Les nouveaux modèles familiaux ou la plus grande mobilité géographique dans le monde du travail – pour ne retenir que ces deux exemples – ont redéfini les impératifs de l'habitation. Aujourd'hui, ceux qui se lancent dans l'aventure de la construction individuelle disposent de davantage d'informations, possèdent plus de connaissances en architecture et en décoration d'intérieur qu'auparavant et surtout savent ce qu'ils veulent – avec exactitude. Ainsi, aux besoins spécifiques répondent des solutions concrètes et personnalisées. De vastes espaces aux fonctions multiples ou des pièces parfaitement pensées pour un usage spécifique, des espaces de travail clairement différenciés des zones de repos et de loisirs, des chambres ouvertes sur le reste de l'habitation ou au contraire isolées dans leur intimité… la demeure contemporaine s'ouvre à toutes les possibilités.

Les résidences présentées dans ce volume font montre d'une grande diversité au niveau des matériaux utilisés, choisis pour s'adapter à leur environnement, plutôt que le contraire. La plupart d'entre elles ont été pensées pour respecter la nature. Les exigences inhérentes au programme architectural, ainsi que la localisation géographique des maisons, contribuent à définir les formes extérieures de la demeure. Des solutions originales et des techniques novatrices sont trouvées pour intégrer l'architecture dans son cadre, ou au contraire pour créer un contraste visuel stimulant, pour créer des ambiances personnelles et des demeures s'adaptant au rythme de vie de chacun. Presque aucune limite n'est imposée à la créativité des architectes et des décorateurs. *Architecture Inspirations* montre des projets équilibrés entre intérieur et extérieur, pour lesquels les lignes de construction et l'agencement revêtent une importance égale. Cet ouvrage présente les dernières tendances de l'architecture résidentielle et de la décoration d'intérieur, propose une multitude de styles susceptibles de constituer une source d'inspiration pour les lecteurs, en vue d'une construction prochaine ou pour transformer un lieu déjà existant. Afin d'identifier facilement les projets correspondant au milieu choisi, les réalisations sont réunies selon leur localisation géographique (ville et périphérie, petits villages, campagne, montagne ou bord de mer).

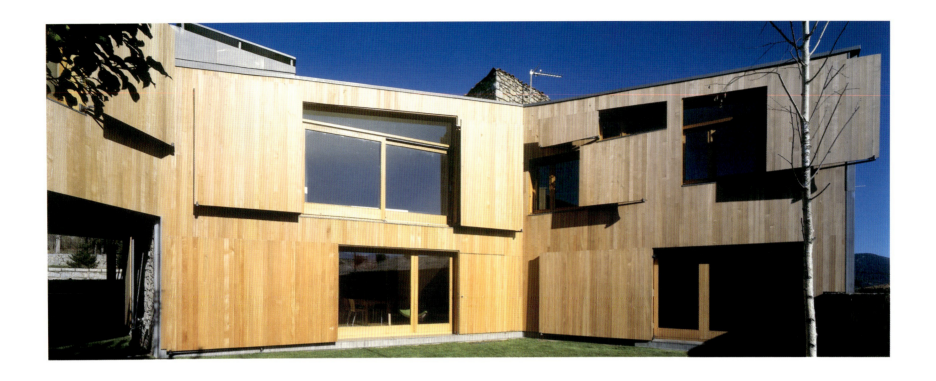

L'architettura residenziale contemporanea è un chiaro riflesso dei cambiamenti sociali ed economici della società. Lasciando da parte le solite case a schiera di alcune urbanizzazioni, in questo settore dell'architettura si sviluppano anche nuove e innovanti costruzioni in cui si può apprezzare come la tecnica e i progressi costruttivi si siano adattati alla creazione di case unifamiliari. Questo libro presenta una ricca e curata selezione di case di tutto il mondo, costruzioni personalizzate ed originali che riflettono le necessità ed i gusti dei proprietari. I nuovi modelli di famiglia o la maggior mobilità lavorativa della gente, per fare solo due esempi, hanno ridefinito le reali necessità di una casa. Attualmente, i proprietari dispongono di maggiori informazioni, più nozioni d'architettura e d'arredamento d'interni, e sanno quello che vogliono più chiaramente. Così dunque, i progetti si costruiscono in funzione delle specifiche necessità, e con soluzioni concrete per ogni cliente. Possiamo trovare, per esempio, grandi finestroni che aprono le case verso l'esterno ed inondando di luce gli interni, ampi spazi per molteplici funzioni, o stanze perfettamente disegnate per un uso specifico. Gli studi o zone di lavoro si possono chiaramente differenziare delle zone riposo, e le stanze da letto diventano gli spazi più intimi delle case. Nella casa contemporanea, vi è spazio per tutte le possibilità.

Le case presentate in questo volume mostrano una gran diversità di materiali che riescono a adattare le costruzioni all'ambiente circostante e non viceversa. Gran parte rispettano l'ambiente e la natura. Le necessità del programma architettonico, insieme all'ubicazione geografica delle case, contribuiscono a definirne le forme esterne. In queste pagine si trovano soluzioni originali e tecniche innovative che, od integrano bene l'architettura nell'ambiente, oppure creano un gran contrasto visivo ed estetico. Qualsiasi opzione è valida e non vi è limite alle creazioni degli architetti e degli arredatori. Le case di "Architecture Inspirations" sono dei progetti integrali in cui sono importanti tanto le linee della costruzione quanto il design dei loro interni. Il libro vuole mostrare le ultime tendenze dell'architettura residenziale e d'interni, proporre stili diversi ed essere fonte d'ispirazione per i lettori. Inoltre, questa selezione può offrire delle idee tanto per la costruzione di una nuova proprietà quanto per un nuovo arredamento di una casa abituale. Soluzioni pratiche, ingegnose ed ardite per creare atmosfere proprie e case che si adattano al ritmo di vita d'ogni persona. La suddivisione in capitoli riunisce i progetti in funzione delle situazioni geografiche (città e periferia, piccoli centri, campagna, montagna o vicino all'acqua) per ottenere una prossimità con il lettore, e per consentirgli di identificarsi con le proposte presentate.

CITY HOUSES

HÄUSER IN DER STADT

CASAS EN LA CIUDAD

MAISONS DE VILLE

CASE IN CITTÀ

Los proyectos de arquitectura urbana que se exponen en este libro son un ejemplo de soluciones innovadoras y experimentales, y ponen de manifiesto la transformación que ha sufrido el concepto de vivienda urbana en los últimos años. Estas construcciones presentan una serie de particularidades específicas marcadas por el entorno. Las normativas y leyes urbanísticas de cada país limitan inevitablemente las posibilidades constructivas, y el ambiente urbano se convierte así en un reto para el arquitecto y para la construcción de viviendas unifamiliares. En la primera fase de la planificación de una vivienda es imprescindible tener en cuenta las necesidades de los propietarios y la superficie edificable de la parcela, normalmente más reducida que en otros lugares como la montaña o el campo. En algunas ocasiones se han realizado remodelaciones y ampliaciones de otras residencias originales, y es aquí donde se muestran las soluciones arquitectónicas de los arquitectos. Las interrelaciones visuales que se crean con el resto de las casas y los edificios del entorno es otro aspecto importante. El resultado visual del conjunto puede resultar más o menos estético, ya sea a través de un gran contraste o gracias a la continuidad con el estilo de los alrededores. En este capítulo, la expresión y la creatividad de los arquitectos se reflejan a través del diseño y la construcción de la vivienda. Las cuestiones referentes a la función específica de cada espacio tampoco se han dejado de lado. Así pues, los proyectos presentados a continuación muestran un excelente equilibrio entre construcción y habitabilidad. Los interiores de estas casas ubicadas en ciudades de todo el mundo responden a unas necesidades muy definidas, propias del estilo de vida urbano y cosmopolita. Las funciones de las estancias están minuciosamente estudiadas y cada una de ellas presenta un diseño que sigue las últimas tendencias, pero sin olvidar la parte funcional. Los nuevos materiales y el mobiliario de este apartado muestran las posibilidades de crear espacios que permitan múltiples usos.

Les projets d'architecture urbains exposés dans ce chapitre présentent des solutions novatrices et expérimentales, qui mettent en évidence la transformation qu'a connu le concept de maison urbaine au cours des dernières années. Ces constructions partagent une série de particularités spécifiques dues à leur environnement. En effet, les normes et législations urbanistiques de chaque pays marquent et délimitent inévitablement les possibilités de construction, le cadre urbain constituant à lui seul un défi pour l'architecte. Lors des études préalables réalisées par les architectes, la superficie constructible disponible constitue le premier cadre de travail ; en ville, elle est souvent, bien sûr, plus réduite qu'à la montagne ou à la campagne. D'ailleurs, la plupart des travaux réalisés portent sur des rénovations ou des extensions d'habitations déjà existantes, ce qui nécessite de la part des architectes ingéniosité et sens de l'harmonie. Les relations visuelles avec les maisons et les immeubles avoisinants constituent un autre aspect important, que ce soit à travers un grand contraste ou le choix d'une esthétique proche.
Les intérieurs de ces maisons répondent à des nécessités propres au style de vie urbain. Les fonctions de chaque pièce sont étudiées minutieusement et présentent les dernières tendances en matière de design. Les nouveaux matériaux et le mobilier choisis permettent de multiples usages. Les projets présentés dans ce chapitre montrent comment arriver à un parfait équilibre entre les contraintes imposées par la situation urbaine – et ce quel que soit le pays concerné – et les choix architecturaux et esthétiques des maîtres d'ouvrage.

I progetti d'architettura in città riportati in questo libro, sono un esempio di soluzioni innovatrici e sperimentali che evidenziano la trasformazione subita nel corso degli ultimi anni dal concetto di casa urbana. Queste costruzioni presentano una serie di particolarità specifiche marcate dall'ambiente circostante. Le normative e le leggi urbanistiche d'ogni paese influiscono e limitano inevitabilmente le possibilità costruttive, e l'ambiente urbano si trasforma in una sfida per l'architetto e per la costruzione di case unifamiliari. All'inizio della pianificazione di una casa è imprescindibile tener conto delle necessità dei proprietari e della superficie edificabile della parcella, normalmente più ridotta rispetto ad altri luoghi come montagna o campagna. In certe occasioni, gli interventi effettuati sono ristrutturazioni ed ampliamenti d'altre case originali, ed è qui che si evidenziano le soluzioni architettoniche degli architetti. Un altro aspetto importante è quello delle interrelazioni visive che si creano con le altre case e gli edifici circostanti. Il complesso visivo che si genera può essere più o meno estetico, o mediante un gran contrasto o grazie alla continuità con gli stili vicini. In questo capitolo l'espressione e la creatività degli architetti si riflette nel design e nella costruzione della casa. Non sono state trascurate le questioni inerenti alla funzione specifica d'ogni spazio. Così, dunque, i progetti presentati a seguire mostrano un eccellente equilibrio tra costruzione ed abitabilità. Gli interni di queste case situate in città di tutto il mondo rispondono a delle necessità molto definite, proprie dello stile di vita urbano e cosmopolita. Le funzioni d'ogni camera, sono state minuziosamente studiate e presentano un design che segue le ultime tendenze, senza dimenticare la parte funzionale. I nuovi materiali e i mobili di questo capitolo mostrano quali siano le possibilità di creare spazi per usi molteplici.

The architectural projects for city houses included in this book exemplify innovative, experimental solutions and highlight the changes our idea of the city home has undergone over the last few years. These spaces present certain location-specific features. Each country's regulations and planning byelaws inevitably determine and limit the scope of construction. Likewise, the urban setting is always a challenge for architects designing single family homes. In the initial stages of home planning, the architect must be familiar with the end user's needs and the dimensions of the plot – which normally permits a smaller construction volume than in other settings such as country or mountain sites. In some cases, the work in hand consists of projects for the renovation or extension of existing homes, which are ideal showcases for professional architectural solutions. Another important aspect are the visual relationships established between a house and any other buildings nearby. The resulting ensemble may be more or less aesthetically pleasing from a visual point of view, through vivid contrast or thanks to stylistic continuity. In this respect, architects' expressiveness and creativity comes through in the design and construction of the home. Moreover, we have not overlooked the specific function of each space. Thus, the projects depicted below exhibit a perfect balance between construction and habitability. The interiors of these city homes located all over the world meet very closely-defined requirements, mirroring an urban, cosmopolitan lifestyle. Each predicted use has been minutely studied, and every room has been designed following state-of-the-art trends to provide fully functional results. New materials and furniture reviewed in this section demonstrate how multiple-use spaces can be formed.

Die architektonischen Beispiele von Stadthäusern, die in diesem Buch vorgestellt werden, zeigen innovative und experimentelle Lösungen und verdeutlichen die Veränderungen, die das Konzept der Stadtwohnung in den letzten Jahren durchgemacht hat. Diese Häuser weisen eine ganze Reihe von Besonderheiten auf, die durch die Umgebung bestimmt sind. Die städtischen Bauvorschriften jedes Landes prägen und begrenzen unvermeidlicherweise die baulichen Möglichkeiten, und die städtische Umgebung wird bei der Errichtung von Einfamilienhäusern zu einer Herausforderung an den Architekten. In der ersten Planungsphase eines Wohnhauses müssen vor allen Dingen die Anforderungen der Kunden und die bebaubare Oberfläche der Parzelle berücksichtigt werden. Normalerweise handelt es sich um kleinere Grundstücke als die auf dem Land. Manchmal werden Umbauten oder Erweiterungen bereits existierender Gebäude durchgeführt, und genau bei dieser Art von Planungen zeigen die Architekten ihr Können und neue architektonische Lösungen. Ein anderer wichtiger Aspekt ist die visuelle Wechselbeziehung, die mit den anderen Häusern der Umgebung geschaffen wird. Das Gesamtbild, das dabei entsteht, kann ästhetisch sehr gelungen oder weniger geglückt sein. Zu einem ästhetisch gelungenen Aussehen tragen oft große Gegensätze oder die Fortsetzung des bereits bestehenden Stils der Umgebung bei. In diesem Kapitel zeigt sich die Ausdrucksstärke und Kreativität der Architekten in der Gestaltung und Bauweise des Hauses. Auch der spezifischen Funktion jedes Raumes wurde Aufmerksamkeit gewidmet. Deshalb zeigen die im folgenden vorgestellten Gebäude, wie man ein perfektes Gleichgewicht zwischen der Gestaltung eines Hauses selbst und seiner Bewohnbarkeit schaffen kann. Die Innenräume dieser Stadthäuser, egal wo auf der Welt sie sich befinden, müssen ganz bestimmte Anforderungen erfüllen, die sich aus dem städtischen und kosmopolitischen Lebensstil ergeben. Die Funktionen jedes Raumes wurden genau analysiert und sie wurden nach den modernsten Trends gestaltet, ohne dass dabei die Funktionalität aus dem Auge verloren wurde. Die neuen Materialien und das Mobiliar in diesem Kapitel zeigen, wie man multifunktionelle Räume schaffen kann.

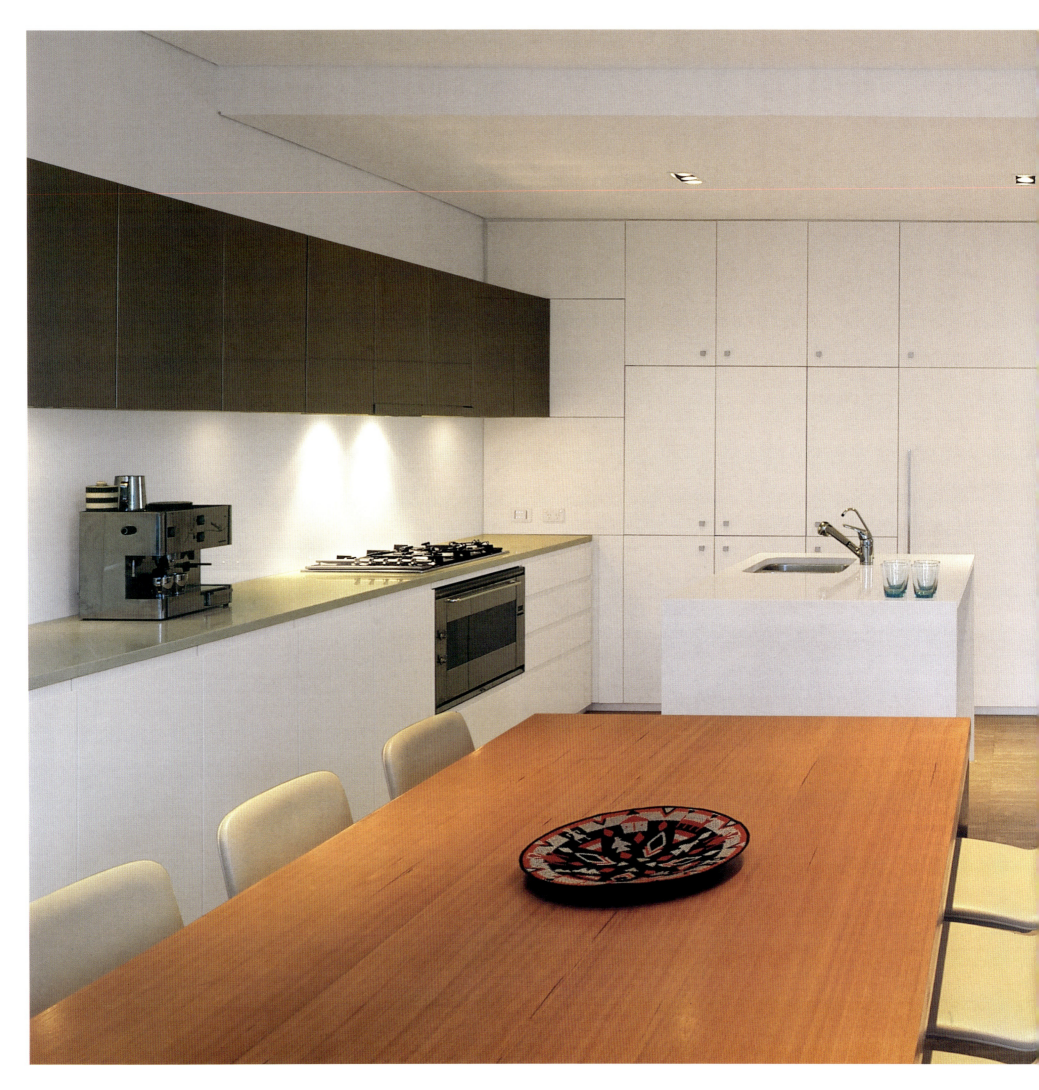

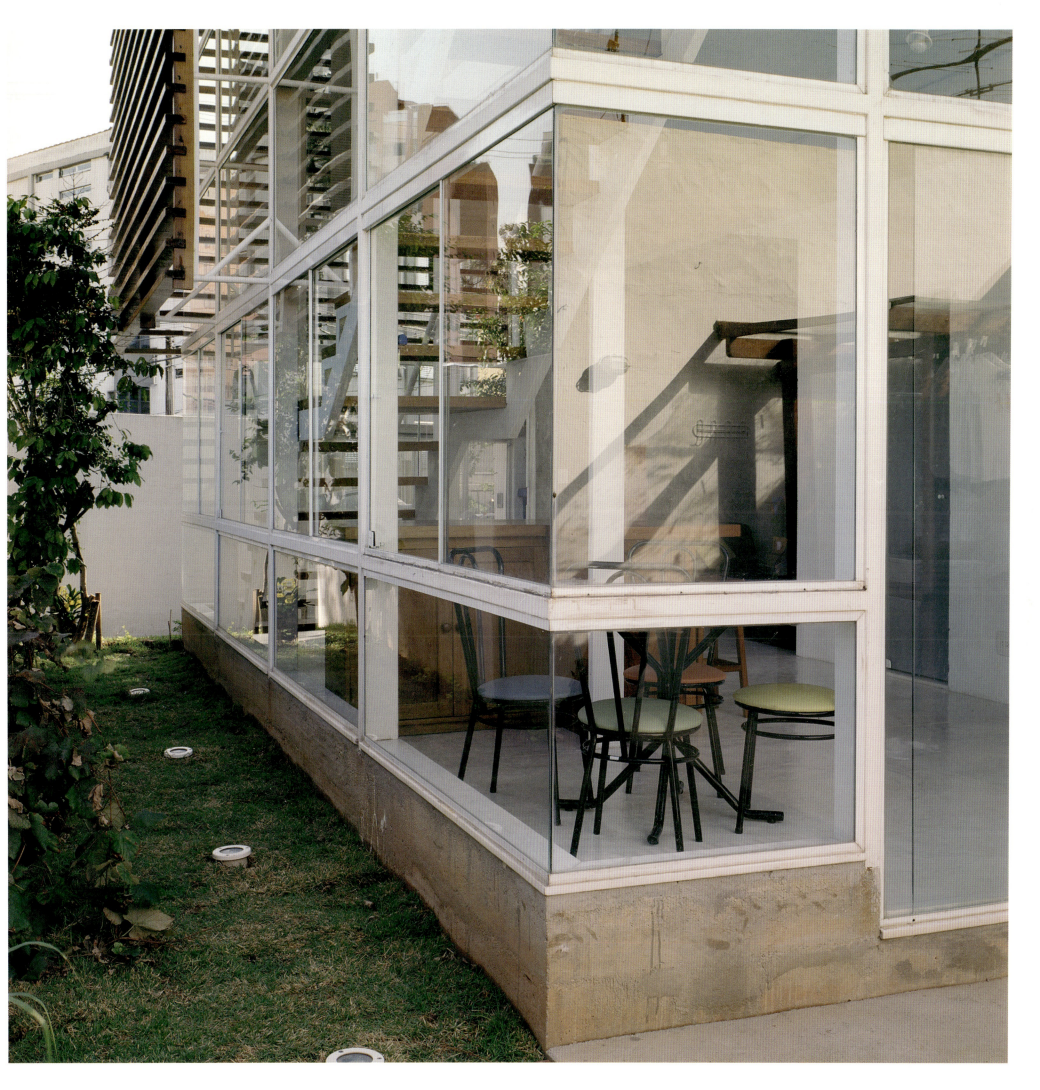

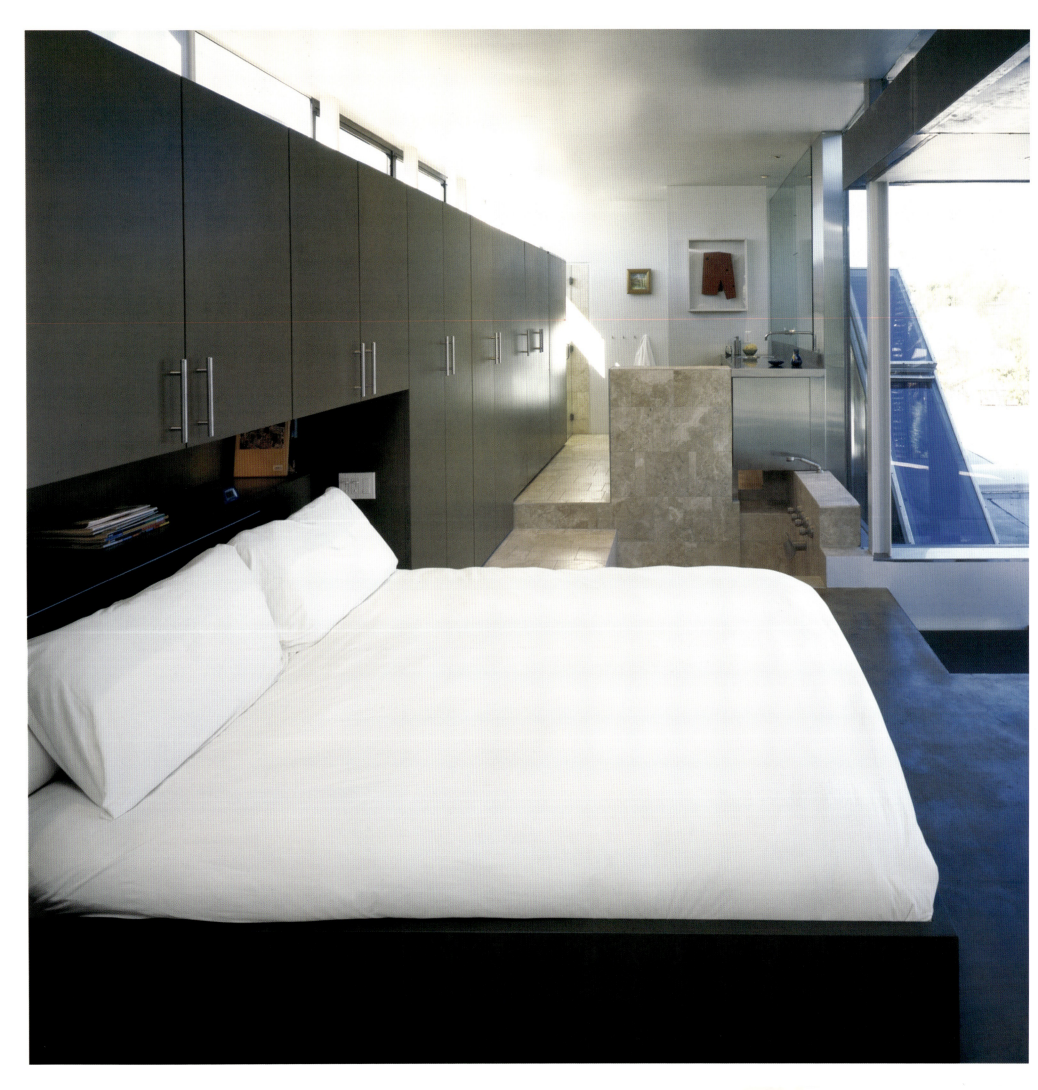

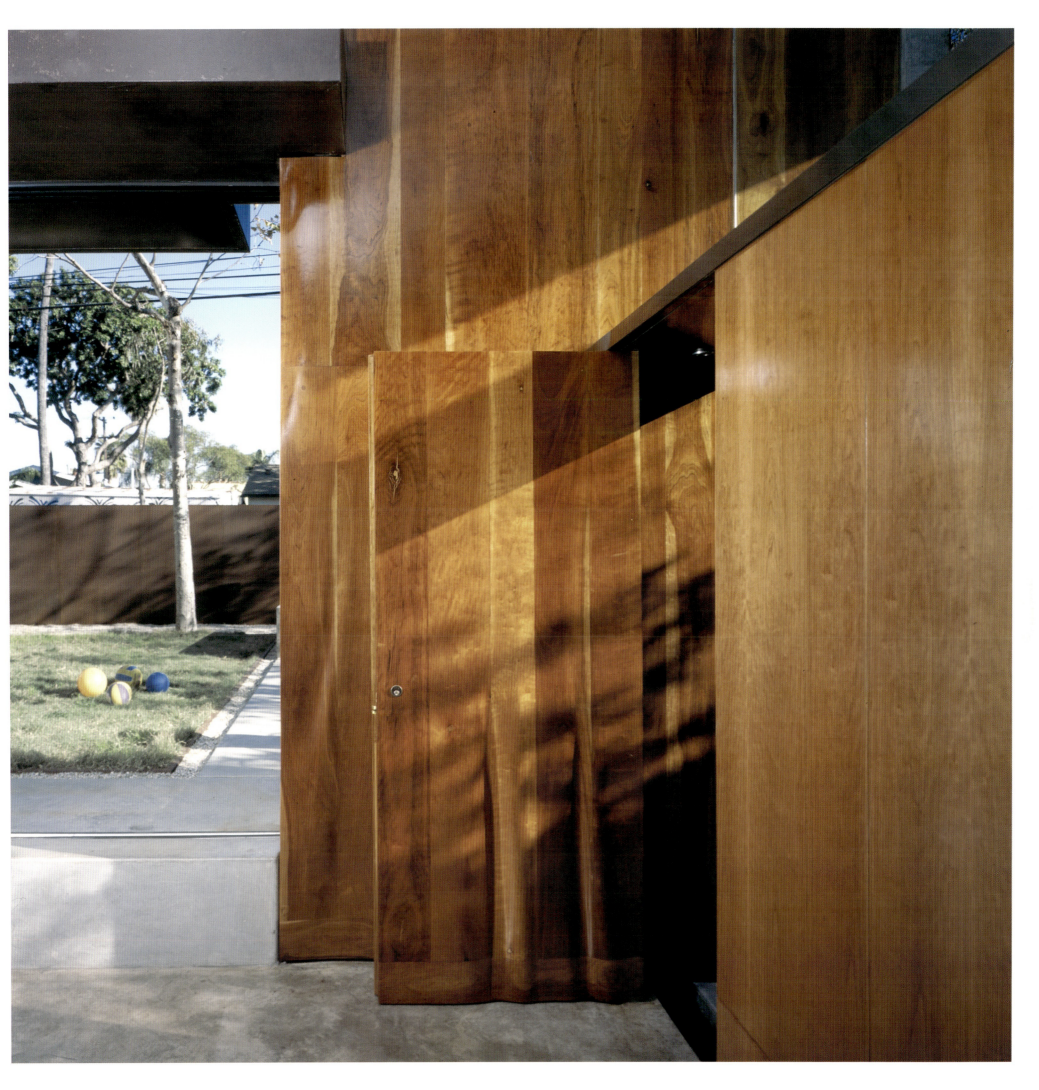

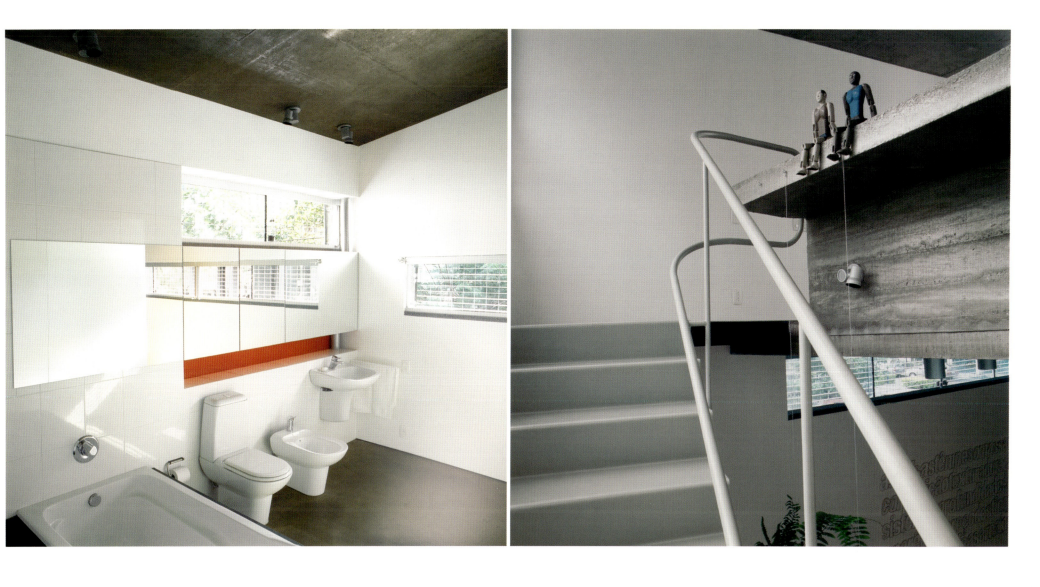

MOUNTAIN HOUSES

HÄUSER IN DEN BERGEN

CASAS EN LA MONTAÑA

MAISONS DE MONTAGNE

CASE IN MONTAGNA

La siguiente selección de casas unifamiliares incluye viviendas ubicadas en regiones montañosas de todo el mundo. Las condiciones climáticas extremas y las oscilaciones de temperatura entre el verano y el invierno definen inevitablemente las características de este tipo de construcciones. Así pues, los materiales de construcción, que deben escogerse con acierto para evitar la degradación de las viviendas, son, además, resistentes y respetuosos con el medio ambiente. El diseño de los interiores debe proteger las viviendas de los cambios de temperatura, del viento, de la radiación solar, de la nieve y de la humedad. Entre las residencias recogidas en esta sección hay casas con grandes ventanales que permiten aprovechar las horas de sol y porches que proporcionan sombra en los calurosos meses estivales. La ubicación apartada y frecuentemente aislada de las casas plantea una serie de dificultades logísticas y constructivas adicionales, como la falta de canalizaciones de agua corriente y la topografía del terreno, que puede llegar a ser extremadamente irregular y compleja. Para resolver estos problemas se han creado originales fórmulas que permiten, además, integrar las viviendas en el paisaje. Ésta es otra de las cuestiones que plantea la arquitectura en la montaña: cómo integrar las viviendas en el entorno natural sin ser agresivos. Algunas casas se fusionan con el entorno y emplean incluso materiales propios de la zona. Éstas siguen, hasta cierto punto, las características de la arquitectura tradicional del lugar. Otros diseños, en cambio, proponen una estética de contraste, más rompedora: son proyectos audaces por el uso del color, las formas atrevidas y los materiales, que aunque no sean propios de la región poseen la misma resistencia que los anteriores. El respeto por el medio ambiente y por la conservación de la naturaleza es un objetivo crucial después de años de turismo y especulación inmobiliaria que han degradado profundamente numerosos entornos naturales. El auge de la conciencia ecológica va acompañado de mejoras constructivas, de nuevos materiales y, en definitiva, de recursos para una construcción sostenible.

La sélection de demeures familiales de ce chapitre inclut des maisons des régions montagneuses de l'ensemble du monde. Les conditions climatiques extrêmes et les variations de température entre l'été et l'hiver marquent inévitablement les caractéristiques de ce type de construction. Ainsi les matériaux doivent être choisis avec soin afin d'éviter la dégradation de la construction ; idéalement, ils allient résistance aux intempéries et respect de l'environnement. Par ailleurs, le design des intérieurs doit protéger les demeures des changements de températures, des effets du vent, des radiations solaires, de la neige et de l'humidité. Ainsi, certaines résidences présentent de grandes baies vitrées afin de tirer parti des heures de soleil, ou des porches pour s'assurer une ombre salutaire lors des mois les plus chauds. La situation de ces maisons – fréquemment isolées – impose souvent d'autres contraintes, tant logistiques qu'architecturales : l'absence d'eau courante ou la topographie du terrain peuvent singulièrement compliquer le projet. Aux architectes de trouver des solutions originales susceptibles d'intégrer la demeure dans le paysage, sans agresser ce milieu fragile et protégé. Certaines maisons cherchent à se fondre dans leur environnement et utilisent même des matériaux propres de la région. Elles suivent aussi, jusqu'à un certain point, les caractéristiques de l'architecture traditionnelle locale. D'autres propositions, en revanche, choisissent une esthétique de contraste, davantage en rupture : il s'agit de projets audacieux de par l'emploi de la couleur, les formes ou les matériaux qui, bien que n'étant pas d'origine autochtone, possèdent toutefois la résistance nécessaire. Le respect et la protection de la nature sont des objectifs essentiels après des années de tourisme et de spéculation immobilière qui ont profondément dégradé beaucoup de sites naturels. La progression d'une prise de conscience écologique s'accompagne de progrès au niveau des normes de constructions, des matériaux et, en définitive, des ressources pour une architecture durable.

La selezione delle case unifamiliari di questo capitolo include case ubicate in regioni montane di tutto il mondo. Le estreme condizioni climatiche e le oscillazioni delle temperature tra l'estate e l'inverno marcano chiaramente le caratteristiche di questa tipologia costruttiva. Così, dunque, la scelta dei materiali costruttivi idonei è importante per evitare il degrado delle case. Materiali che devono essere estremamente resistenti ma non aggressivi con l'ambiente. Il design degli interni deve proteggere le case dalle temperature oscillanti, dagli effetti del vento, le radiazioni solari, la neve e l'umidità. Tra le case di questa sezione, ve ne sono alcune con grandi finestroni che sfruttano al meglio le ore di sole, o con dei porticati che garantiscono l'ombra durante i caldi mesi estivi. L'ubicazione appartata e frequentemente isolata delle case crea una serie di difficoltà logistiche e costruttive aggiunte, come l'assenza di allacci per l'acqua corrente, o la topografia di un terreno che può arrivare ad essere molto irregolare e complesso. Per risolvere questi problemi sono state create delle originali formule che consentono, inoltre, di integrare le case nel paesaggio. Questo è un altro dei problemi dell'architettura di montagna: come integrare le case nella natura senza essere aggressivi. Alcune delle case s'integrano con l'ambiente, ricorrendo addirittura ai materiali propri della zona e, sino ad un certo punto, si seguono le caratteristiche dell'architettura tradizionale del luogo. Altri design, invece, optano per un'estetica di contrasto, più innovatrice: sono dei progetti audaci per l'uso del colore delle forme ardite e dei materiali, che pur non essendo tipici della regione hanno la loro stessa resistenza. Il rispetto dell'ambiente e la tutela della natura è un obiettivo cruciale dopo anni di turismo e di speculazione immobiliare, responsabili del degrado di molti ambienti naturali. L'auge della coscienza ecologica si accompagna da miglioramenti costruttivi, da nuovi materiali e, in definitiva, da risorse per una costruzione sostenibile.

The selection of single family homes offered in this chapter includes residences built in mountainous regions all over the world. Extreme climate conditions and variations in winter and summer temperatures necessarily define the characteristics of these constructions. Thus, highly resistant and environmentally friendly building materials have to be selected. Interior design must incorporate protection from extreme temperature variations and the damaging effects of wind, sun, snow and damp. The residences illustrated in this section include houses with large glazed surfaces to absorb warmth from the sun's rays or porches to provide shade during the hot summer months. Isolation is one of the problems plaguing this type of home, as it brings additional logistic and constructive difficulties such as the absence of water mains or the inaccessibility of the terrain. To overcome these obstacles, some very original formulas have been proposed which, at the same time, contribute further in blending these homes into the landscape. This is precisely one of the difficulties arising with mountain architecture: how to fuse a building inconspicuously into the landscape. Some of the homes reviewed morph with their surroundings; in many cases, these are built from local materials and local architectural uses are largely applied. Other models again opt for a much bolder, contrasting approach, with audacious use of colour, forms and materials which despite not being obtained locally are equal in terms of durability. Respect towards nature and the environment has become a fundamental premise, after many years of tourism and speculative practices that led to the degradation of many natural spaces. Growing ecological awareness goes hand in hand with improved building methods, new materials and – most importantly – the necessary resources for sustainable construction.

In diesem Kapitel werden Einfamilienhäuser gezeigt, die sich in Gebirgsregionen überall auf der Welt befinden. Die extremen klimatischen Bedingungen und die hohen Temperaturunterschiede zwischen Sommer und Winter prägen unvermeidlich diese Art von Gebäuden. So muss das Baumaterial sehr sorgfältig ausgewählt werden, damit es diesen Klimaschwankungen gut standhält. Nur sehr widerstandsfähige Materialien eignen sich, aber sie sollten sich auch gut in die Umgebung einfügen. Auch die Innenräume der Häuser müssen vor Temperatur-schwankungen, vor Wind, Sonne, Schnee und Feuchtigkeit geschützt werden. Wir zeigen Häuser, die große Fenster haben, durch die viel Sonne einfällt, und Veranden, die in den heißen Sommermonaten Schatten spenden. Aufgrund der abgelegenen und isolierten Lage treten bei diesen Häusern eine Reihe von Schwierigkeiten logistischer Natur auf, auch haben sie oft sehr viele Anbauten. Manchmal ist keine Kanalisation für fließendes Wasser vorhanden oder die Geländeform kann sehr unregelmäßig und komplex sein. Um diese Probleme zu lösen, wurden sehr originelle Vorschläge geschaffen, die die Häuser außerdem in die Landschaft einfügen. Das eben ist das andere architektonische Problem, das sich im Gebirge stellt, wie integriert man das Haus am besten in die Umgebung, ohne dass es aggressiv wirkt. Manche der Häuser scheinen mit der Umgebung zu verschmelzen und sind mit den Materialien der Umgebung gebaut. Oft richtet man sich bis zu einem gewissen Punkt nach der typischen, traditionellen Architektur des Ortes. Andere Häuser sind dagegen so gestaltet, dass sie einen starken ästhetischen Gegensatz hervorrufen, der in die Landschaft eindringt. Manche sind in gewagten Farben gehalten, andere haben ungewöhnliche Formen oder es wurden besondere Materialien benutzt, die zwar nicht aus der gleichen Region stammen, aber ebenso widerstandsfähig sind. Eines der wichtigsten Ziele bei der Errichtung von Häusern im Gebirge ist es, die Umwelt und Natur zu schonen, denn die vielen Jahre Tourismus und Immobilienspekulationen haben viele Zonen stark geschädigt. Da sich die Gesellschaft ihrer ökologischen Verpflichtung immer bewusster wird, hat sich auch der Bausektor verändert. Man arbeitet mit neuen Materialien und Mitteln, um umweltgerechtere Häuser zu errichten.

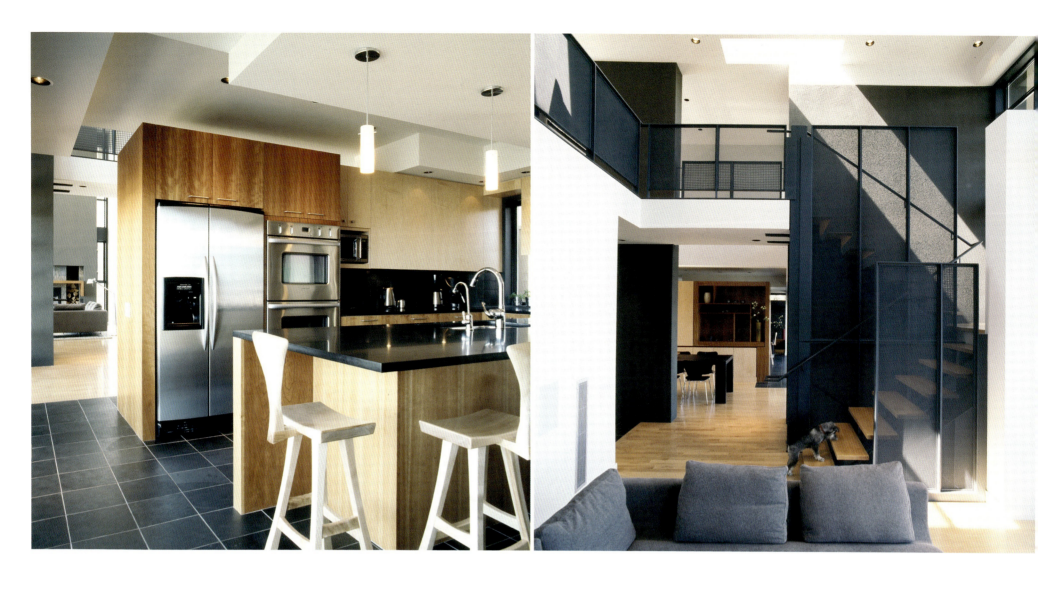

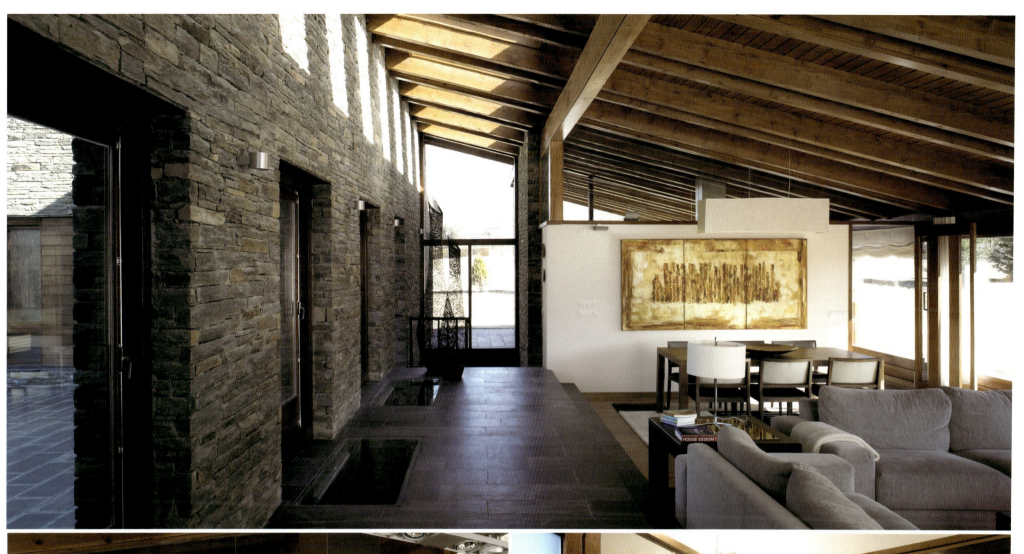

HOUSES IN SMALL TOWNS

HÄUSER IN DÖRFERN

CASAS EN PUEBLOS

MAISONS DE VILLAGE

CASE DI PAESE

En los pueblos pequeños la arquitectura presenta unas características especiales que se deben al ritmo de vida rural, más pausado que en las ciudades. La tranquilidad que emana de los paisajes que los rodean y las diferentes actividades económicas que se realizan en ellos delimitan el tipo de viviendas que se construye. Las construcciones modernas se mezclan así con un entorno tradicional de casas modestas, que conviven a su vez con otras más lujosas, construidas en el pasado para los habitantes más influyentes de las poblaciones. Algunas regiones han experimentado en el pasado éxodos de población hacia las ciudades o las zonas industriales, lo que ha provocado un empobrecimiento y abandono de los municipios. Por el contrario, en otras regiones las zonas rurales han resurgido con fuerza gracias al turismo rural. Algunas casas son, en realidad, segundas residencias de personas originarias de estos lugares. Entre casas cargadas de historia y pequeños barrios que han crecido gracias a la bonanza económica, descubrimos una arquitectura contemporánea, moderna y que se adapta con gran naturalidad a este medio. Los arquitectos asumen el reto de crear viviendas personalizadas y originales, con un perfil propio y que, además, se integren con las residencias de los alrededores. Las casas entre medianeras o las construcciones de nueva planta en solares irregulares son solamente dos ejemplos de la diversidad arquitectónica que se puede encontrar. En las residencias unifamiliares que se muestran a continuación se incluyen soluciones específicas adaptadas a los requisitos de los propietarios. En algunos proyectos, las alturas y los volúmenes de las casas son el resultado de la adaptación a los espacios disponibles; en otros, se han creado espacios privados al aire libre, como patios y jardines. Algunas de las viviendas, situadas en pequeños pueblos costeros, han sido especialmente diseñadas para poder disfrutar de las vistas y para aprovechar al máximo la luz natural. Asimismo, la sencillez de los interiores define unas casas pensadas para el disfrute de cada rincón.

Dans les petits villages, l'architecture présente des caractéristiques spéciales, dues au rythme de vie rural, plus posé que celui des villes. La tranquillité qui émane des paysages environnants et les différentes activités économiques locales délimitent le type de demeure qui se construit. Les constructions modernes se mêlent ainsi à un cadre traditionnel de maisons modestes, coexistant avec d'autres plus luxueuses, héritage du passé des habitants les plus influents de la population. Certaines demeures sont parfois des résidences secondaires de personnes originaires de la région. Certaines zones ont connu, par le passé, des exodes vers les villes ou les zones industrielles, provoquant un appauvrissement et un abandon des communes rurales. D'autres, au contraire, vivent une véritable renaissance grâce à des activités comme le tourisme rural ou les sports d'aventure. Entre maisons chargées d'histoire et petits quartiers s'étant développés grâce à la croissance économique, nous découvrons une architecture moderne, qui s'adapte avec beaucoup de naturel à son environnement. Les architectes relèvent le défi de créer des maisons personnalisées, originales et qui s'intègrent parfaitement aux résidences alentour. Les maisons mitoyennes ou les constructions sur plusieurs niveaux pour s'adapter à un terrain irrégulier sont peu représentées dans ce chapitre, essentiellement consacré aux résidences familiales individuelles.

Nei paesini l'architettura presenta delle caratteristiche speciali imposte dal ritmo della vita rurale, più tranquillo di quello cittadino. La tranquillità che sprigionano i paesaggi che li circondano e le diverse attività economiche che vi si svolgono, influiscono sul tipo di casa che vi si costruisce. Le costruzioni moderne si mescolano così in un ambiente tradizionale di case modeste che convivono con altre più lussuose, costruite in passato dagli abitanti più influenti dei centri. In passato, alcune regioni hanno sofferto importanti esodi verso le città o verso le zone industriali, provocando un impoverimento ed un abbandono dei municipi. In altre, invece, le zone rurali sono risorte con forza grazie ad attività come il turismo rurale o lo sport d'avventura. Alcune case sono in realtà delle seconde residenze di persone originarie di questi centri. Tra case piene di storia e piccoli quartieri sorti grazie al boom economico, troviamo un'architettura contemporanea, moderna, che si adatta con gran naturalità a quest'ambiente. Gli architetti accettano la sfida di creare case personalizzate ed originali, con profili propri, capaci, inoltre d'integrarsi con le case circostanti. Le case intermedie, o le costruzioni di un nuovo piano in parcelle irregolari, sono solo due degli esempi delle varietà architettoniche che vi si possono trovare. Nelle case unifamiliari presentate a continuazione, s'includono soluzioni specifiche per le necessità dei proprietari. In alcuni progetti l'altezza ed i volumi delle case sono il risultato dell'adattamento agli spazi disponibili; in altri, sono stati creati spazi privati all'aperto come cortili e giardini. Alcune delle case, situate in paesini della costa, sono state concepite per fruire delle viste e sfruttare al massimo la luce naturale. Inoltre, la semplicità degli interni definisce delle case pensate per godersi ogni angolo.

Small village architecture displays a number of special characteristics that are the result of unhurried rural lifestyles that unfold at an easier pace than life in the city. The tranquillity of the landscape and the various economic activities pursued put certain limitations on the type of housing built. Modern constructions merge with a traditional entourage of modest homes side by side with grander ones erected in past times by influential citizens. Some regions suffered population losses, when massive emigration towards major cities or industrial districts caused villages to become impoverished or, in some cases, deserted. On the other hand, some rural areas have made a healthy comeback thanks to tourism and adventure sports. Some houses are in fact second residences for former inhabitants of these villages. The primitive houses, seeped in history, and the new quarters that have sprung up around them thanks to booming economic conditions, have spawned a new brand of contemporary architecture, modern and fully adapted to its environment. Architects have risen to the challenge of formulating original, highly personalised homes with unique features which nevertheless fit in naturally with other buildings in the vicinity. Houses built between party walls or new houses built on oddly-shaped plots are but two examples of the infinite variety of architectural situations that arise. The single family homes on these pages show different specific solutions to owners' needs. In some projects, height and volume are the result of adapting to the available space; in others, private open-air spaces have been achieved in patios and gardens. Some houses in small coastal towns have been designed to take maximum advantage of any views and natural lighting. Likewise, interior simplicity is the first principle upon which to build a home in which every square inch is engineered for comfort and enjoyment.

In kleinen Dörfern weist die Architektur besondere Kennzeichen auf, die auf den ländlichen Lebensrhythmus zurückzuführen sind. Es herrscht mehr Ruhe als in den Städten. Die umgebende Landschaft strahlt Gelassenheit aus und der Haustyp, der gebaut wird, richtet sich nach den wirtschaftlichen Aktivitäten, die in der Umgebung zu finden sind. Moderne Häuser vermischen sich mit einer traditionellen Umgebung, die von bescheidenen Häusern geprägt ist, neben denen sich luxuriösere Bauten befinden, die in der Vergangenheit für die einflussreicheren Bewohner der Dörfer errichtet wurden. In einigen Regionen wanderte die Bevölkerung in die Städte oder Industriegebiete ab, so dass die Gemeinden verarmten und verlassen wurden. Im Gegensatz dazu hat in anderen ländlichen Gebieten ein starker Aufschwung stattgefunden, der auf Aktivitäten wie den Tourismus auf dem Lande oder das Angebot an Abenteuersportarten zurückzuführen ist. Einige der Häuser sind in Wirklichkeit Ferienhäuser der Menschen, die in diesen Dörfern geboren wurden. Zwischen diesen Häusern, die auf eine lange Geschichte zurückblicken und kleinen Vierteln, die aufgrund des wirtschaftlichen Wohlstands entstanden sind, finden wir eine zeitgemäße und moderne Architektur, die sich sehr natürlich an diese Umgebung anpasst. Die Architekten haben die Herausforderung angenommen, persönliche und originelle Häuser zu planen, die einen eigenen Stil haben und außerdem zu den umgebenden Gebäuden passen. Reihenhäuser und neue Gebäude auf unregelmäßig geformten Grundstücken sind nur zwei Beispiele für die architektonische Vielfalt, die zu finden ist. Alle Einfamilienhäuser, die im folgenden gezeigt werden, zeichnen sich durch spezifische Lösungen aus, die für die besonderen Anforderungen der Eigentümer gefunden wurden. Bei einigen dieser Häuser ergab sich die Höhe und die Form aus dem zur Verfügung stehenden Raum, bei anderen wurden private Räume im Freien wie Höfe und Gärten geschaffen. Einige der Häuser in kleinen Dörfern an der Küste wurden so entworfen, dass man den Blick genießen und das Tageslicht maximal ausnutzen kann. Einfache Innenräume definieren Häuser, die man bis auf den letzten Winkel genießen kann.

247

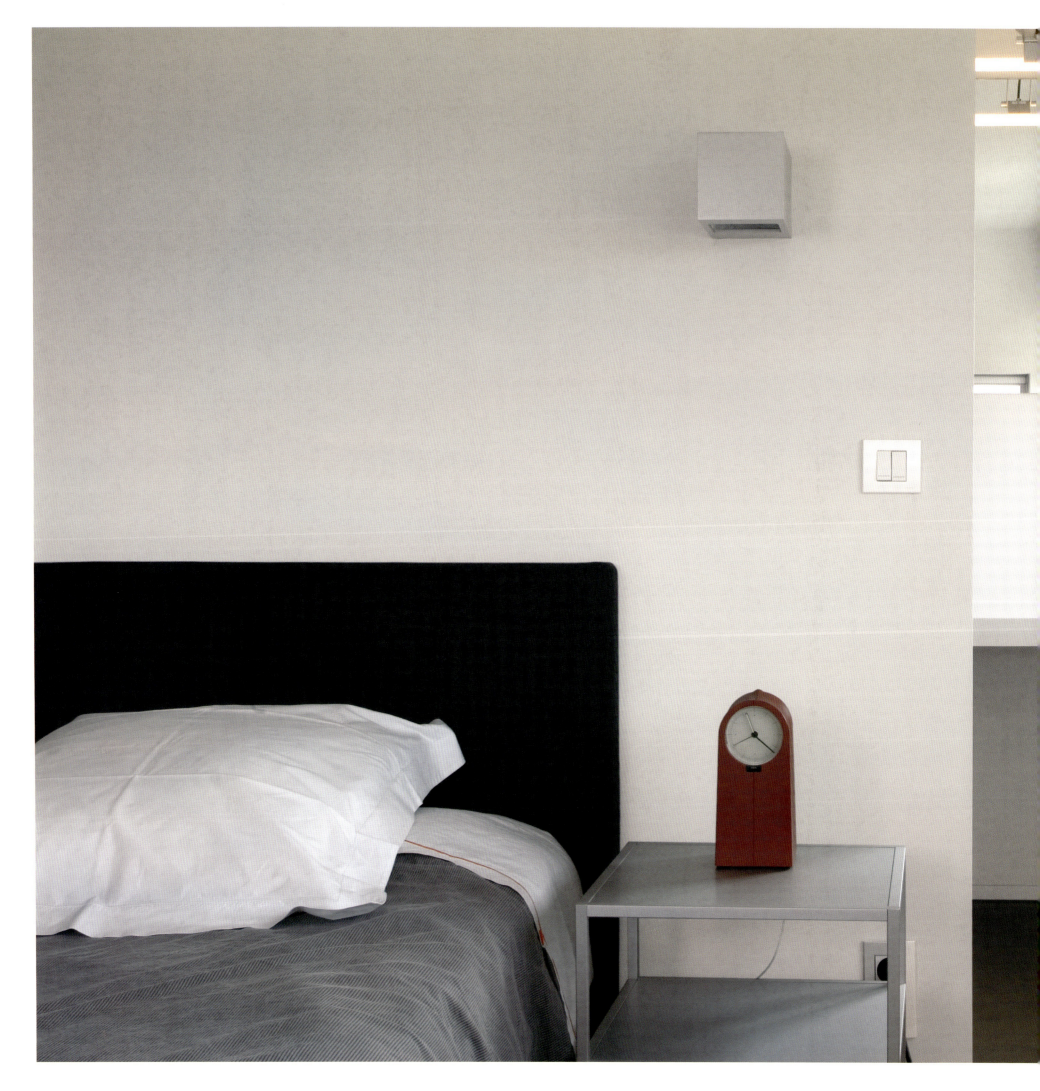

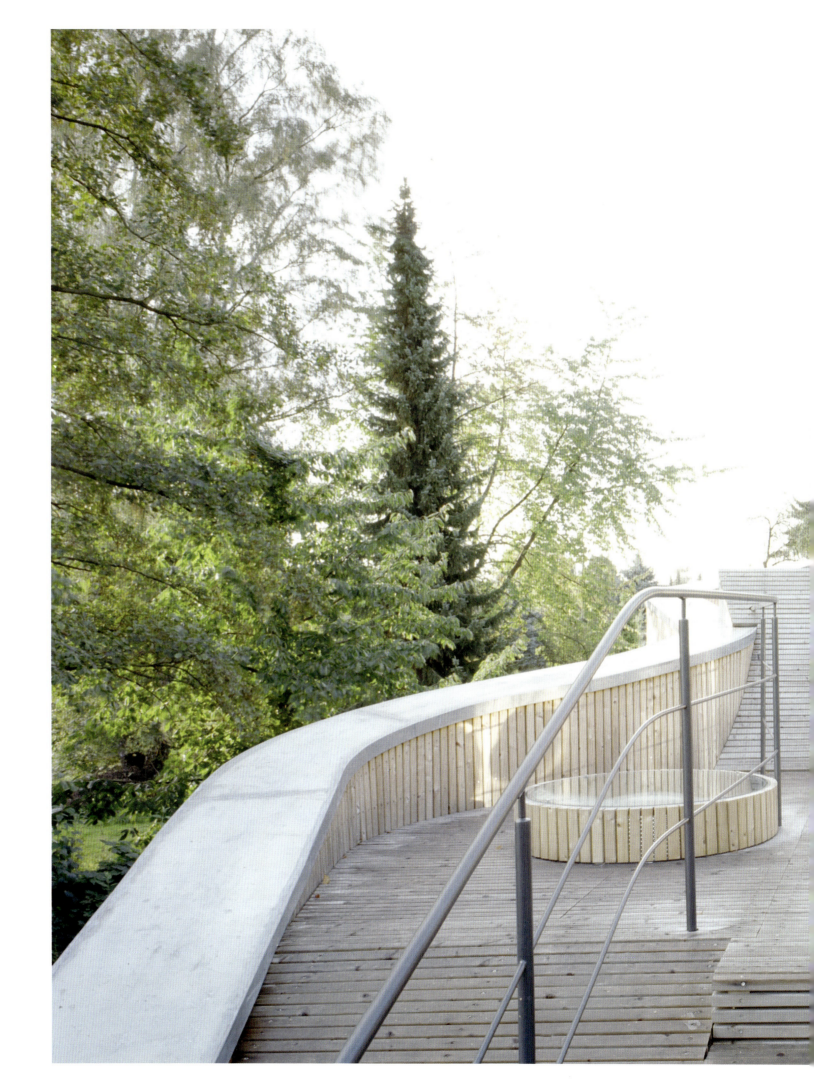

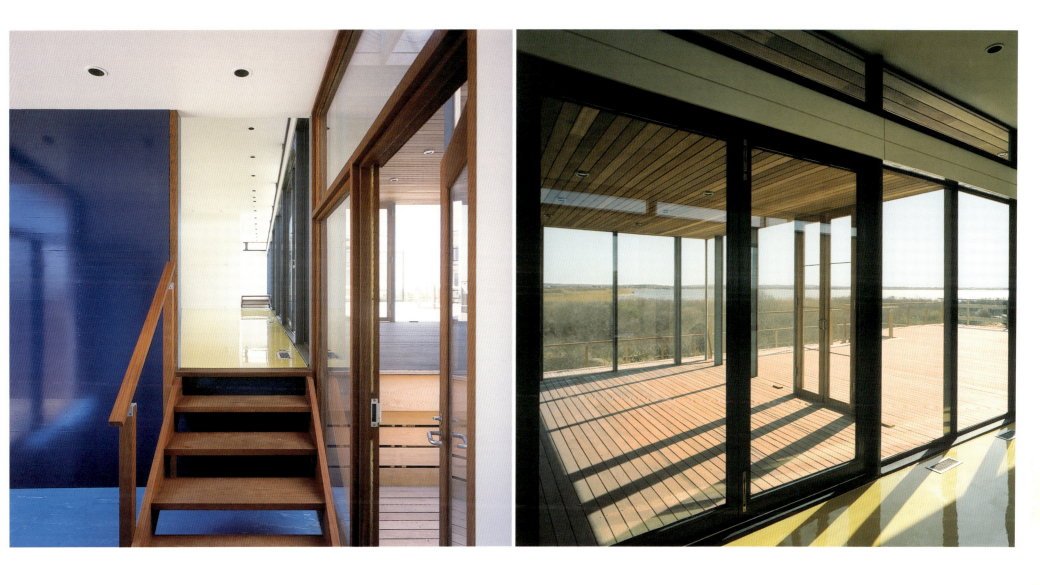

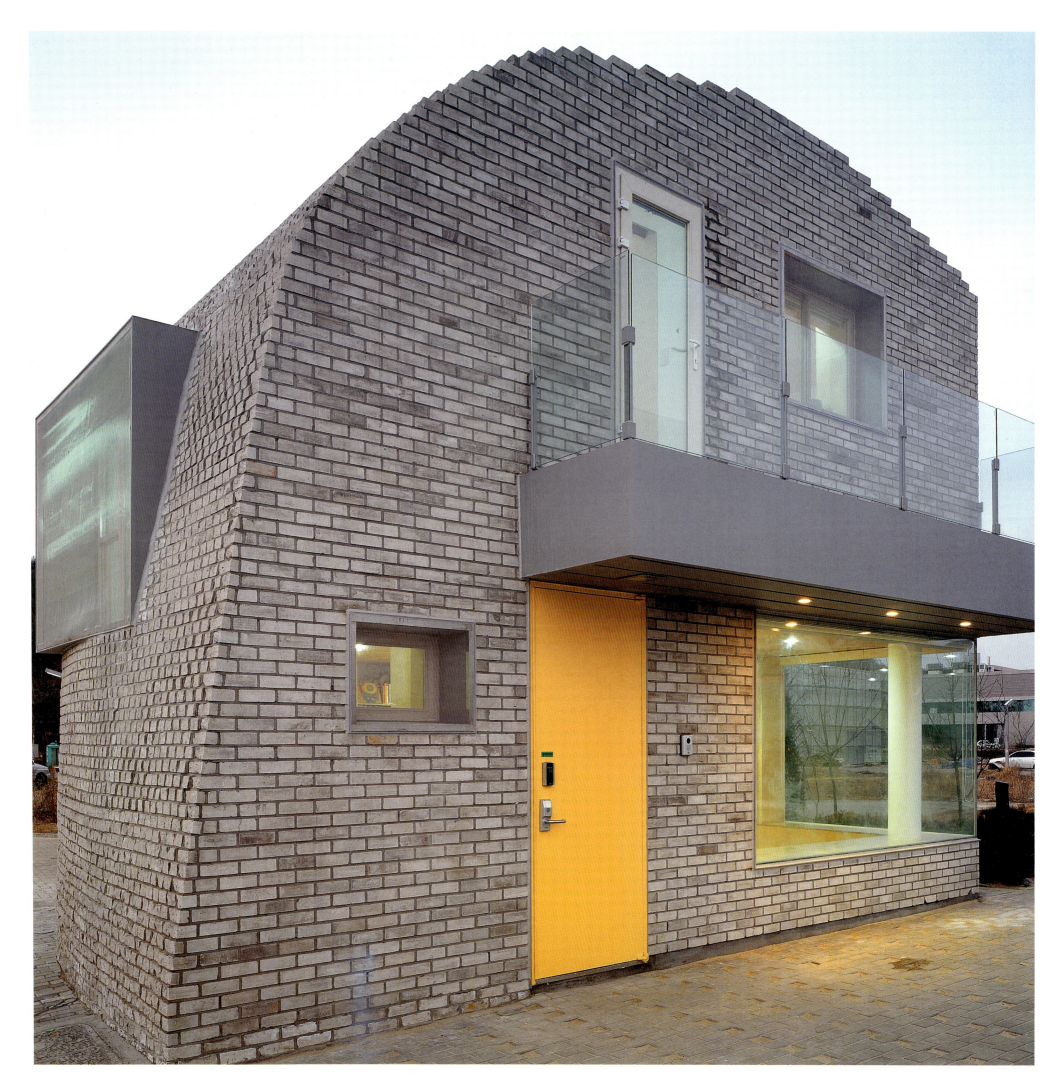

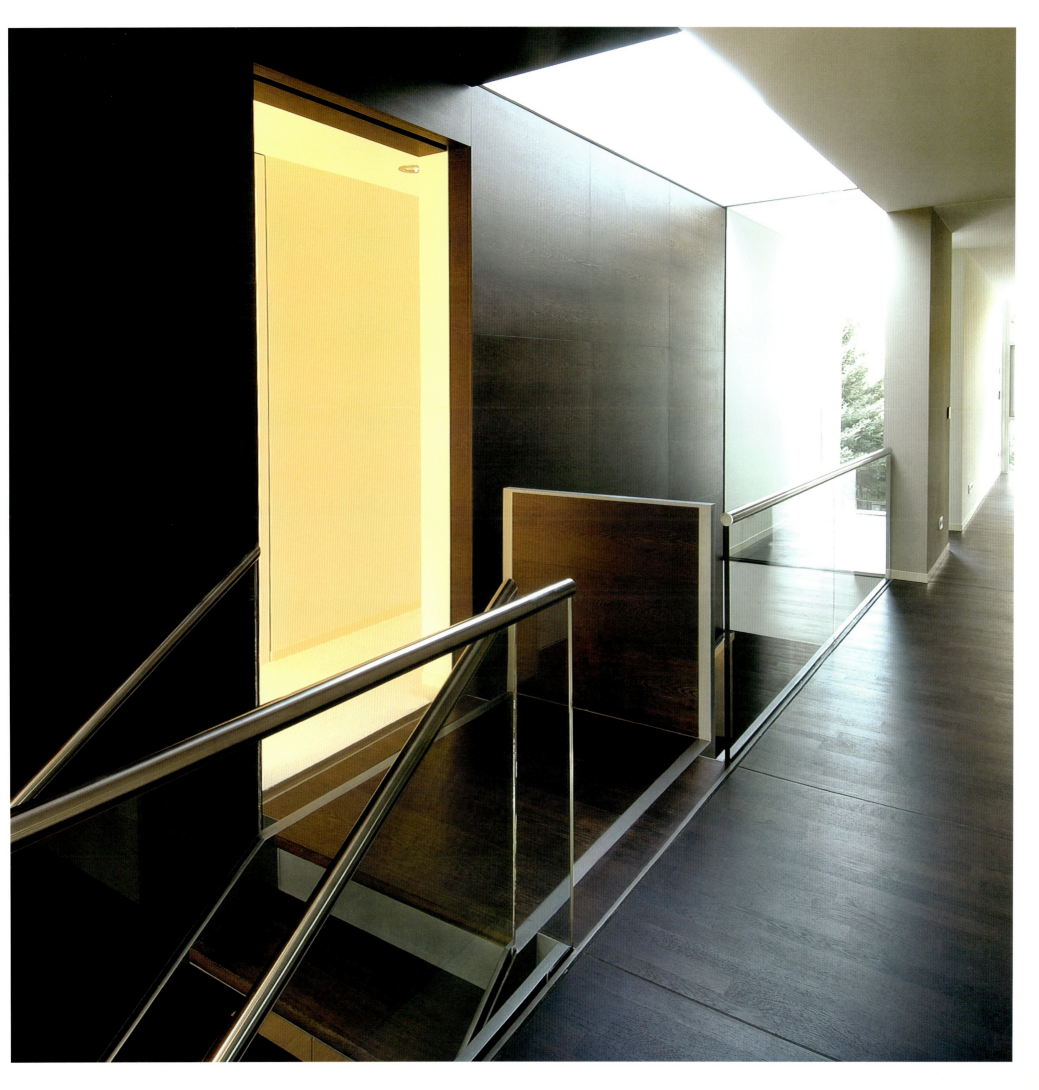

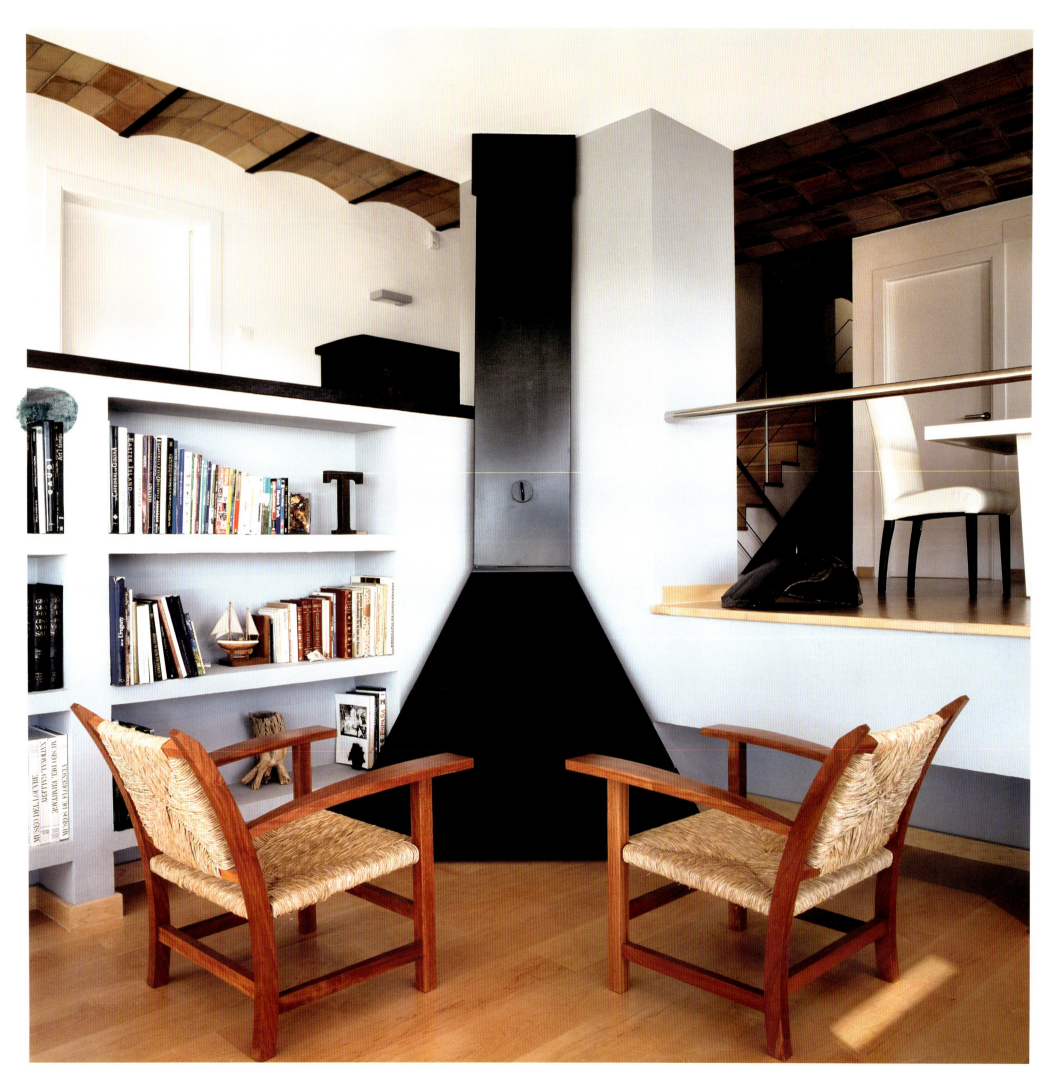

COUNTRY HOUSES

HÄUSER AUF DEM LAND

CASAS EN EL CAMPO

MAISONS DE CAMPAGNE

CASE IN CAMPAGNA

Normalmente, la arquitectura en el campo se define como la antítesis de la arquitectura en la ciudad. El ritmo de vida y los entornos naturales son tan diferentes que hacen pensar en estilos de vida completamente opuestos. Pero hablar de casas en el campo puede resultar muy ambiguo, pues el concepto mismo de "campo" varía en función de diferentes criterios. En este volumen se incluyen residencias unifamiliares emplazadas en diversos lugares y con características y soluciones arquitectónicas distintas. Aunque las viviendas de las ciudades y de la periferia tienen puntos en común, presentan, sin embargo, numerosas diferencias. Por lo tanto, deben mostrarse separadamente dependiendo de la ubicación. Las casas en pueblos no tienen por qué encontrarse necesariamente en la montaña: es precisamente la tipología de núcleo urbano donde se hallan lo que las hace diferentes. Las viviendas reunidas en este capítulo no están ni en pueblos ni en la montaña, ni tampoco en ciudades, sino en una especie de tierra de nadie. Se pueden encontrar residencias unifamiliares situadas junto a campos de cultivo, en suaves colinas o en valles poco profundos. Además, los paisajes que envuelven las casas de campo son habitualmente menos extremos que los entornos montañosos. Así pues, esta arquitectura está condicionada por el entorno natural pero de un modo distinto, ya que la topografía suele ser menos problemática y esto define la línea de las construcciones. Asimismo, las condiciones climáticas son menos extremas, lo que condiciona también la elección de los materiales de construcción. La preocupación por el medio ambiente es un objetivo y un estímulo para la mayoría de los arquitectos, y los materiales bioclimáticos no sólo se utilizan para obtener un mayor confort, sino también para lograr un notable ahorro de energía. Las siguientes viviendas presentan formas originales y únicas, materiales escogidos conscientemente para formar conjuntos llenos de fuerza y funcionalidad. Los interiores muestran un amplio abanico de posibilidades para los lectores, pues estos proyectos constituyen ejemplos y guías para las propias viviendas. Las últimas tendencias en decoración se fusionan con la comodidad y muestran un estilo de vida perfectamente adaptado al entorno.

Normalement, l'architecture à la campagne se définit comme l'antithèse de celle des villes. Les rythmes de vie et les cadres naturels sont si différents qu'ils peuvent apparaître comme diamétralement opposés. Mais le fait de parler de maisons de campagne peut s'avérer passablement ambigu. En effet, la conception même de la « campagne » varie selon plusieurs critères. Le présent volume inclut des résidences familiales aux emplacements multiples et dont les caractéristiques et solutions architecturales sont distinctes. Bien que les maisons en ville et en banlieue présentent des points communs, elles affichent toutefois nombre de différences. De ce fait, elles doivent être abordées séparément en fonction de l'endroit qui les accueille. Les maisons de villages ne se trouvent pas nécessairement en montagne : c'est précisément la typologie du noyau urbain où elles se trouvent qui les rend si différentes. Les maisons de ce chapitre proposent des demeures qui ne sont ni dans des villages, ni en montagne, pas plus qu'en ville. Il s'agit plutôt d'une sorte de « no man's land ». Nous pouvons rencontrer des maisons familiales situées à côté d'un champ cultivé, sur des collines en pente douce voire des vallées peu profondes. En outre, les paysages qui se laissent contempler depuis ces maisons de campagne sont habituellement moins extrêmes que ceux des environnements montagneux. De la sorte, cette architecture est conditionnée par un cadre naturel mais d'une manière distincte. La topographie pose normalement moins de difficultés ce qui transparaît dans les lignes architecturales. Par ailleurs, les conditions climatiques sont moins exigeantes, comme cela se révèle notable pour les matériaux de construction. La préoccupation pour le milieu ambiant est un objectif et un aiguillon pour la majorité des architectes. Pour cette raison, les matériaux bioclimatiques sont non seulement utilisés pour assurer un confort optimal mais aussi pour bénéficier d'économies d'énergies significatives. Les demeures de ce chapitre présentent des formes originales et uniques, des matériaux choisis consciencieusement pour former des ensembles riches de leur force et de leur fonctionnalité. Les intérieurs proposent une vaste palette de possibilités pour les lecteurs. Ces projets sont ainsi de véritables exemples et guides pour leur propre demeure. Les tendances ultimes en décoration fusionnent avec l'esprit pratique pour manifester un style de vie en harmonie parfaite avec son environnement.

Normalmente, l'architettura in campagna si definisce come l'antitesi dell'architettura di città. Il ritmo di vita e gli ambienti naturali sono così diversi da far pensare a stili di vita completamente opposti. Parlare, però, di case di campagna può essere molto ambiguo, poiché il concetto di campagna varia in funzione di vari criteri. In questo volume s'includono le case unifamiliari di vari luoghi e con diverse caratteristiche e soluzioni architettoniche. Sebbene le case delle città e della periferia abbiano dei punti in comune, presentano, comunque, numerose differenze, e debbono dunque essere presentate separatamente in funzione del luogo in cui si trovano. Le case di paese non devono trovarsi in montagna: è proprio la tipologia del nucleo urbano in cui si trovano a renderle diverse. Le case di questo capitolo non sono né di paese né di montagna, ma nemmeno di città, una specie, dunque, di terra di nessuno. Vi sono case unifamiliari situate vicino a campi coltivati, su morbide colline o in valli poco profonde. Inoltre, i paesaggi che si possono godere dalle case di campagna sono abitualmente meno estremi di quelli montani. Pertanto, quest'architettura è condizionata dalla natura circostante ma in un modo diverso, perché la topografia è normalmente meno problematica e ciò definisce le linee costruttive. Inoltre, le condizioni climatiche sono meno estreme, cosa che condiziona anche i materiali costruttivi. La preoccupazione per l'ambiente è un obiettivo ed uno stimolo per la gran parte degli architetti, ecco dunque che i materiali bioclimatici, non solo si usano per avere un maggior comfort, ma anche per ottenere un considerevole risparmio energetico. Le case di questo capitolo hanno delle forme originali ed uniche, con materiali scelti in modo cosciente per creare dei complessi pieni di forza e funzionalità. Gli interni mostrano una vasta scelta di possibilità per i lettori, perché questi progetti sono esempi e guida per le proprie case. Le ultime tendenze dell'arredamento si sposano con la comodità, mostrando uno stile di vita perfettamente adattato all'ambiente.

Normally, the architecture of country homes is by definition the antithesis of urban architecture. Pace and surroundings are so different in the country that one can safely speak of entirely different lifestyles. The term country houses, however, can be misleading since the concept of 'country' may vary enormously depending on the criteria applied. In this volume you will find a range of single family homes in different locations, with different features and architectural solutions. Though city and suburban homes have many characteristics in common, they nevertheless present clear differences, which is why we include each in separate chapters based on location. Village houses are not necessarily in hilly country or in the mountains, and it is precisely the kind of urban location that makes them different. Homes in this chapter are neither in villages nor out in the mountains, nor in cities either: they are in a sort of no man's land. Single family homes may be next to farmland, on a gentle hillside or in a deep valley. The views country homes generally enjoy over the surrounding landscapes are never as breathtaking as those from houses built in mountainous terrain. This style of architecture, therefore, is conditioned by its natural surroundings in a different way, since these are topographically speaking rarely a problem and this comes through in constructive style. Likewise, less extreme climate conditions open greater possibilities for building materials. Respect for the environment is both an aim and a stimulus for most architects, who favour bioclimatic materials for greater comfort and considerable energy savings. The homes shown in this chapter display unique, original layout schemes and the materials have been selected deliberately to forge powerful and functional compositions. These projects are intended as a guide for readers to take example from such a wide repertory of possibilities for their own homes. The latest home decoration trends are clearly comfort-oriented creating a style that is perfectly compatible with country life.

Normalerweise wird die ländliche Architektur als eine Art Antithese zur städtischen definiert. Der Lebensrhythmus und die umgebende Natur sind so anders, dass man gleich an einen völlig gegensätzlichen Lebensstil denken muss. Wenn man jedoch von Häusern auf dem Land redet, beschreitet man ein sehr doppeldeutiges Feld, da das Konzept Land von verschiedenen Kriterien abhängig ist und sehr unterschiedlich sein kann. In diesem Band werden Einfamilienhäusern an verschiedenen Orten und mit sehr verschiedenen Eigenschaften und sehr vielfältige architektonische Lösungen vorgestellt. Obwohl die Häuser in den Städten und am Stadtrand Gemeinsamkeiten haben, weisen sie auch zahlreiche Unterschiede auf. Deshalb zeigen wir sie getrennt und je nach Standort. Die Häuser in Dörfern müssen sich nicht unbedingt in den Bergen befinden. Eigentlich ist es die Art von Siedlung, Dorf oder Stadt, in der sie sich befinden, die ihren Charakter bestimmt. Die Häuser, die in diesem Kapitel gezeigt werden, stehen weder in einem Dorf noch im Gebirge. Sie befinden sich auch nicht in einer Stadt, sondern in so einer Art Niemandsland. Es werden Einfamilienhäuser gezeigt, die neben einem Feld stehen, in einer sanften Hügelkette oder einem tiefen Tal. Außerdem sind die Landschaften, die diese Häuser umgeben, normalerweise sanfter als Berglandschaften. So wird auch diese Architektur von der Natur bestimmt, die sie umgibt, aber auf eine andere Weise, da die Geländeoberfläche, die die Linien eines Gebäudes definiert, meist unproblematisch ist. Auch die klimatischen Bedingungen sind weniger extrem, was sich auf die verwendeten Baumaterialien auswirkt. Die meisten Architekten sind heutzutage dazu übergegangen, umweltschonend zu bauen. So werden bioklimatische Baumaterialien verwendet, die die Häuser nicht nur komfortabler machen, sondern auch sehr viel Energie einsparen. Die Häuser, die in diesem Kapitel vorgestellt werden, sind originell und einzigartig. Die Baumaterialien wurden sorgfältig ausgewählt, um kraftvolle und funktionelle Gebäude zu schaffen. Auch die Gestaltung der Innenräume ist sehr vielfältig. Sie können dem Leser als Inspiration und Beispiel für die Gestaltung ihrer eigenen Häuser dienen. Die letzten Dekorationstrends werden in eine komfortable und angenehmen Wohnumgebung integriert, und es wird ein Lebensstil gezeigt, der sich perfekt an die Umgebung anpasst.

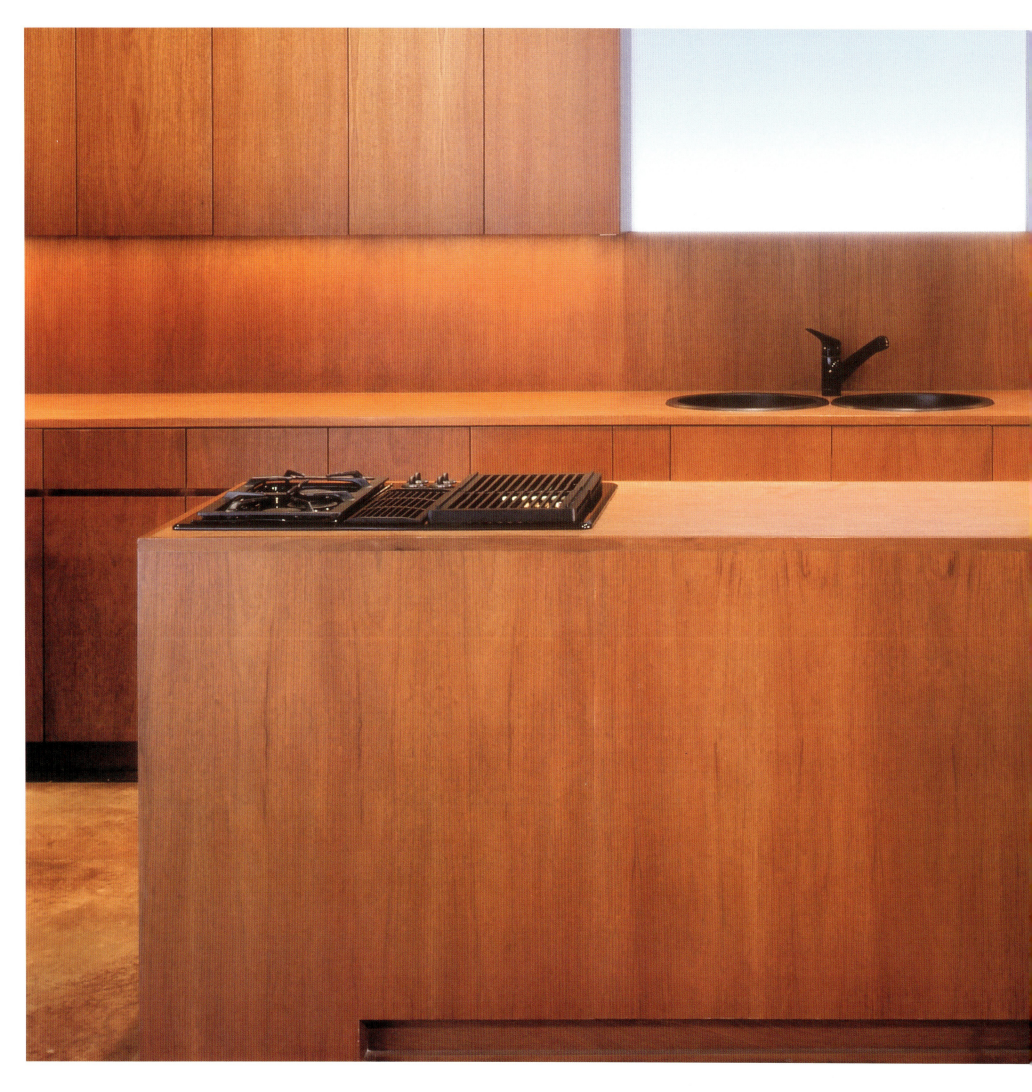

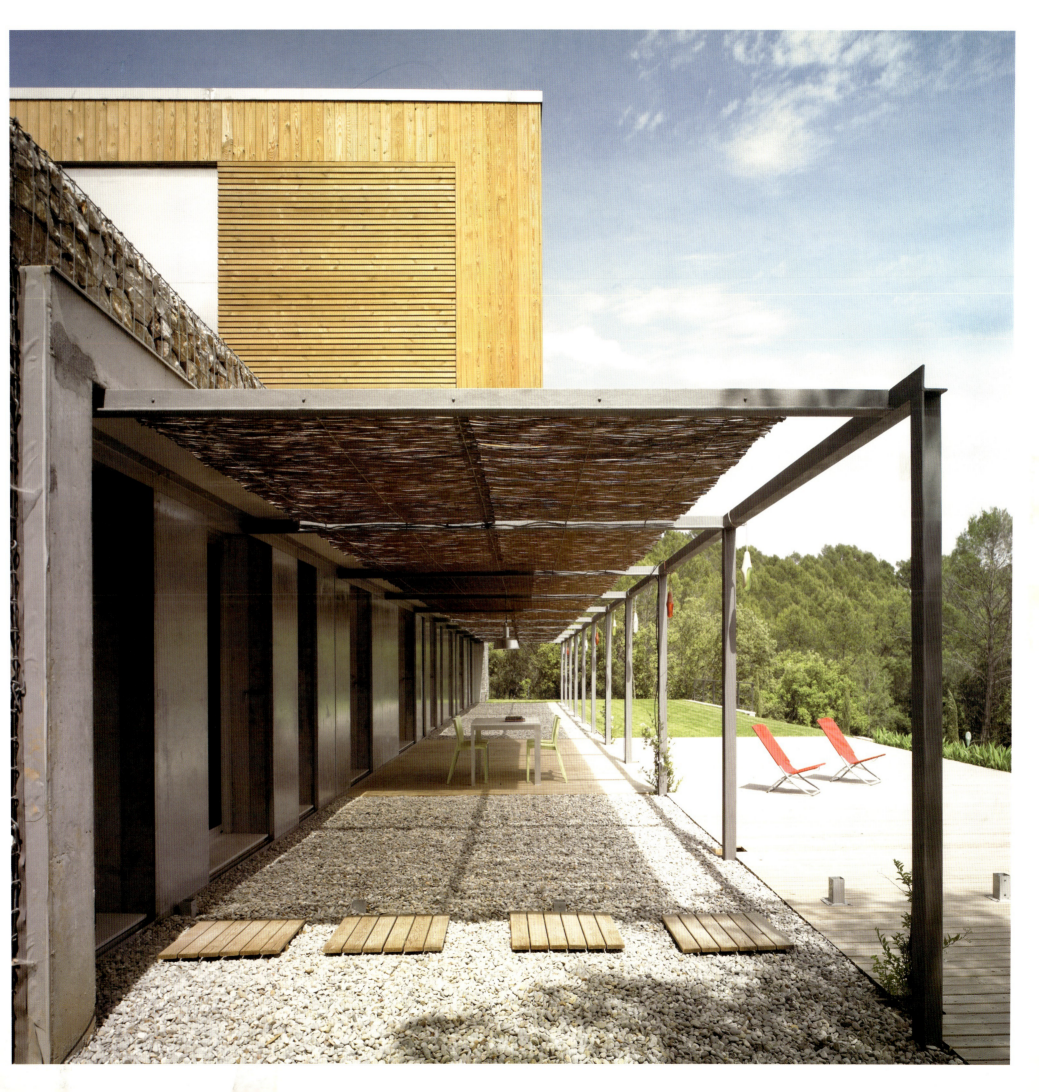

SUBURBAN HOUSES

HÄUSER AM STADTRAND

CASAS EN LA PERIFERIA

PAVILLONS DE BANLIEUE

CASE IN PERIFERIA

Vivir en la periferia de una gran ciudad ofrece numerosas ventajas, pues en realidad se vive entre dos mundos. La proximidad de las ciudades permite seguir un ritmo y un estilo de vida urbano, pero, al mismo tiempo, la distancia que separa estas zonas de las urbes permite disfrutar de espacios más amplios, de una mayor tranquilidad y de una mejor calidad de vida. Las residencias unifamiliares situadas en la periferia de las grandes ciudades pertenecen a un tipo de arquitectura difícil de clasificar. Existen casas de todo tipo, es cierto, pero lo más frecuente es que la palabra periferia evoque las casas del extrarradio que se ubican en las pequeñas ciudades dormitorio. Hablar de viviendas en las afueras nos hace pensar inmediatamente en urbanizaciones con interminables hileras de casas clónicas, desprovistas de personalidad. Sin embargo, este volumen selecciona residencias que son la antítesis de estas ideas preconcebidas. Las posibilidades expresivas son aquí mayores que en las ciudades, donde las normativas urbanísticas pueden limitar la libertad de los arquitectos, y es posible diseñar residencias con mucha más personalidad y que tengan en cuenta las necesidades de los propietarios. Las viviendas que aparecen a continuación son aparentemente más simples y sus líneas arquitectónicas, más claras y, por lo tanto, más comprensibles. Esta simplicidad se combina con el juego de volúmenes para crear casas con fuerza. La diversidad de los materiales constructivos, así como la variedad de entornos que las acogen, permite mostrar una amplia variedad de diseños. Asimismo, la luz desempeña un papel importante al generar juegos que definen las estancias interiores y los perfiles del exterior. Se hace evidente que estas viviendas son extremadamente personalizadas y que responden a los amplios conocimientos de sus propietarios sobre arquitectura e interiorismo. La coherencia entre el exterior de las casas y su diseño interior crea conjuntos con carácter que muestran la evolución de la arquitectura residencial contemporánea.

Vivre dans la banlieue d'une grande ville peut offrir bien des avantages. Mais la vie se déroule en fait entre deux mondes. La proximité de la ville permet de continuer à suivre le rythme et le style de vie urbains tout en profitant d'espaces plus amples, d'une plus grande tranquillité et d'une meilleure qualité de vie. Les résidences familiales situées à la périphérie des grandes villes appartiennent à un type d'architecture difficile à classifier, car tous les types de maisons coexistent. Cependant, le mot « périphérie » évoque le plus souvent les maisons de banlieue s'invitant dans les petites cités dortoirs. Parler des maisons de banlieue ravivent l'idée de lotissements avec leurs files interminables de maisons clonées, dépourvues de toute personnalité. Ce chapitre présente des résidences bien différentes de ces clichés. Les réalisations rassemblées ici sont apparemment plus simples, avec des lignes architecturales plus claires et, par conséquent, plus compréhensibles. Les possibilités expressives sont ici plus conséquentes qu'en ville, où les normes urbanistiques peuvent limiter la liberté des architectes. La diversité des matériaux de construction, ainsi que la variété des environnements les accueillant, permettent de présenter un large éventail de design. Il devient ainsi possible de concevoir des habitations à la personnalité plus affirmée et tenant compte des impératifs de leurs propriétaires. Elles sont l'expression manifeste de l'ampleur des connaissances des maîtres d'ouvrage en architecture et en décoration d'intérieur. Par ailleurs, la lumière revêt une importance cruciale en générant des jeux qui définissent les pièces à l'intérieur et les profils à l'extérieur. La cohérence entre l'extérieur de la maison et son design intérieur crée des ensembles de caractère, qui démontrent l'évolution de l'architecture résidentielle contemporaine.

Vivere in periferia di una gran città può presentare molti vantaggi, poiché in realtà si vive tra due mondi. La prossimità delle città consente di seguire un ritmo lavorativo ed uno stile di vita urbano, ma al contempo, la distanza che separa queste zone dell'urbe consente di godersi spazi più ampi, una maggior tranquillità ed una miglior qualità di vita. Le case unifamiliari situate alla periferia delle grandi città, appartengono ad un tipo d'architettura difficile da classificare. Vi sono case di tutti i generi, ma la cosa più frequente è che la parola periferia evochi case extra urbane ubicate spesso in città dormitorio. Quando si parla di case fuori città, si pensa a comprensori con interminabili file di case cloniche prive di personalità. In questo volume si vogliono mostrare delle case che sono l'antitesi di queste idee preconcette. Le possibilità espressive sono qui maggiori, rispetto alle città, in cui le norme urbanistiche possono limitare gli architetti, e si può dunque disegnare delle case con molta più personalità, tenendo conto delle necessità dei proprietari. Questi esempi mostrano delle case in apparenza più semplici, con linee architettoniche più chiare e, dunque, più comprensibili. Tale semplicità si abbina al gioco dei volumi per creare case con forza. La diversità dei materiali costruttivi delle case e la varietà degli ambienti circostanti in cui sono ubicate, consente di mostrare una vasta scelta di design. Inoltre, la luce svolge un ruolo importante creando dei giochi che definiscono le stanze interne ed i profili esterni. Evidentemente, queste case molto personalizzate e rispondono alle profonde conoscenze d'architettura e di design dei proprietari. La coerenza tra gli esterni delle case ed il loro design interno, crea degli abbinamenti di carattere che rappresentano l'evoluzione dell'architettura residenziale contemporanea.

Living in the suburbs of a large city can have many advantages, since here one benefits from both worlds: closeness to the city means access to urban work patterns and living standards, while the distance from the city centre makes it possible to enjoy more space, greater tranquillity and a higher quality of life. Single family homes in suburban areas are very difficult to fit into any known architectural category. These homes are of many different types, it is true, but on the whole the term 'suburban' evokes dormitory town spread. Suburban housing conjures up images of never-ending rows of cloned, characterless houses. In these pages, we have tried to compile a selection of houses that will break down this preconceived idea. The amazing scope for expression is in fact far greater here than in the city, where town-planning regulations impose severe limitations on architects, and there is freedom to design residences with bubbling personalities that meet every single one of their owners' needs. In the examples we have included here are homes that appear disarmingly simple, with clear-cut lines revealing their architectural values. Such simplicity combines with artful arrangement of volumes to produce compelling homes. The diversity of building materials and the different location for each of these homes has allowed us to portray a very wide cross-section of current designs. Similarly, light plays a leading role in giving definition to interior spaces and exterior profiles. It becomes clear that these highly personalised dwellings are the result of the owners' extensive knowledge of architecture and interior design. The relationship between exteriors and inner spaces has given rise to buildings of great character, the expression of contemporary residential architecture.

Das Leben am Stadtrand kann viele Vorteile haben, da man sich zwischen zwei Welten befindet. Da die Stadt sehr nah liegt, folgen die Arbeit und der Lebensstil einem städtischen Rhythmus, aber gleichzeitig herrscht aufgrund der Entfernung zur Stadt mehr Ruhe und man hat eine bessere Lebensqualität. Die Einfamilienhäuser am Rand der großen Städte sind architektonisch schwer einzuordnen. Es gibt Häuser jeder Art, aber am häufigsten erinnert das Wort Vorort an die typischen Häuser der Schlafstädte der Außenbezirke. Man denkt an die unendlichen Reihen von identischen Häusern ohne eigene Persönlichkeit. In diesem Buch werden Häuser vorgestellt, die das genaue Gegenteil zu diesem Vorurteil darstellen. Die Ausdrucksmöglichkeiten sind in den Vororten größer als in den Städten, in denen die Bauvorschriften die Architekten stark einengen. Man kann in den Vorstädten Häuser mit einem starken Eigencharakter bauen, die genau auf die Anforderungen ihrer Eigentümer zugeschnitten sind. Wir zeigen Häuser mit klaren und somit verständlichen architektonischen Linien, die anscheinend sehr einfach sind. Diese Einfachheit wird mit einem Spiel mit Formen kombiniert, durch das ein kraftvoller Gesamtausdruck entsteht. Die Verschiedenartigkeit der Konstruktionsmaterialien der Häuser und der Umgebungen, in denen sie sich befinden, lässt eine sehr große Vielfalt von Gestaltungsmöglichkeiten zu. Ebenso spielt das Licht eine wichtige Rolle, es entstehen Effekte, die die Innenräume und die äußeren Formen bestimmten. Es wird deutlich, dass diese Häuser sehr persönlich gestaltet sind und dass ihre Eigentümer umfassende architektonische und innenarchitektonische Kenntnisse besitzen. Durch die Kohärenz zwischen dem Äußeren und dem Inneren dieser Häuser entsteht ein Gesamtbild, das die Entwicklung der Wohnhausarchitektur der heutigen Zeit zeigt.

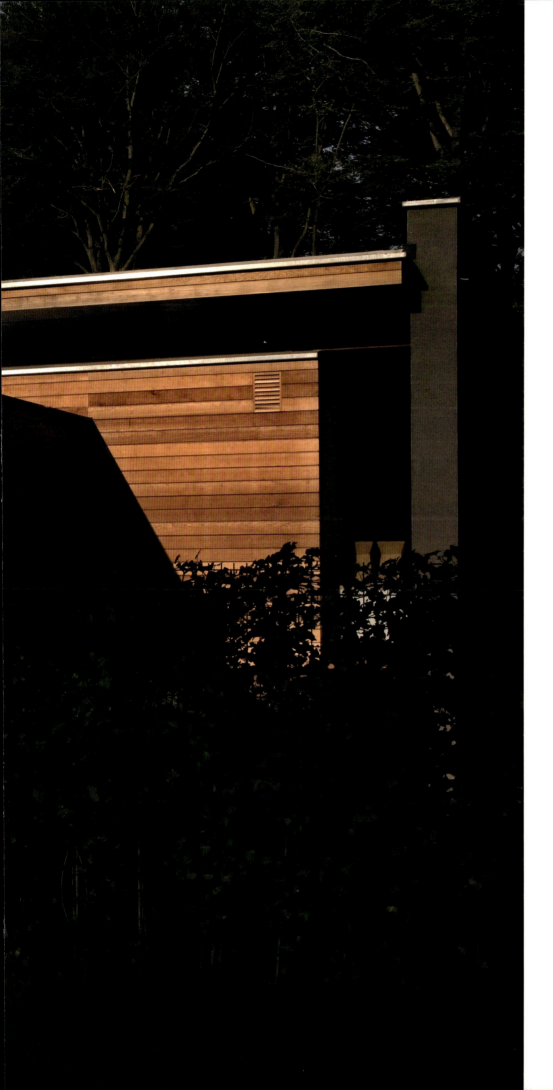

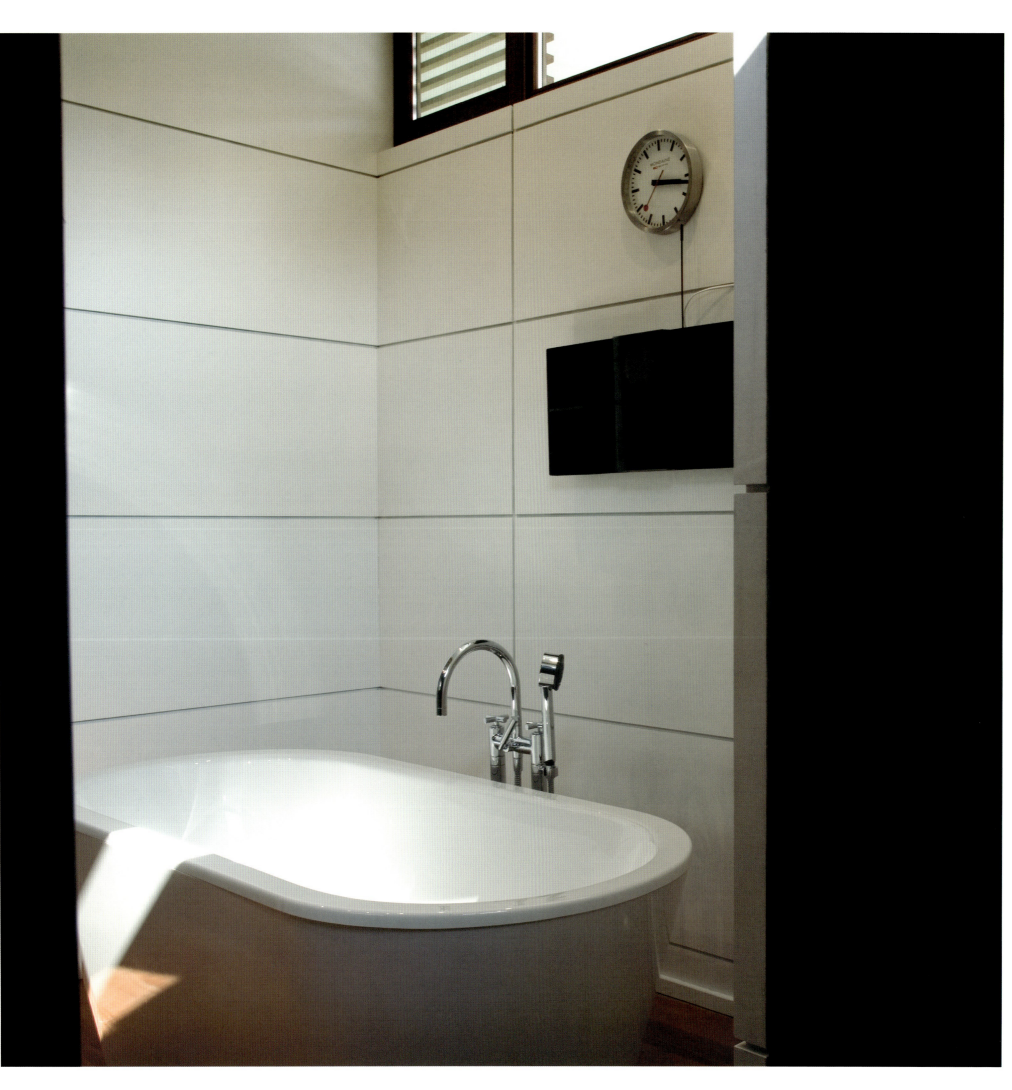

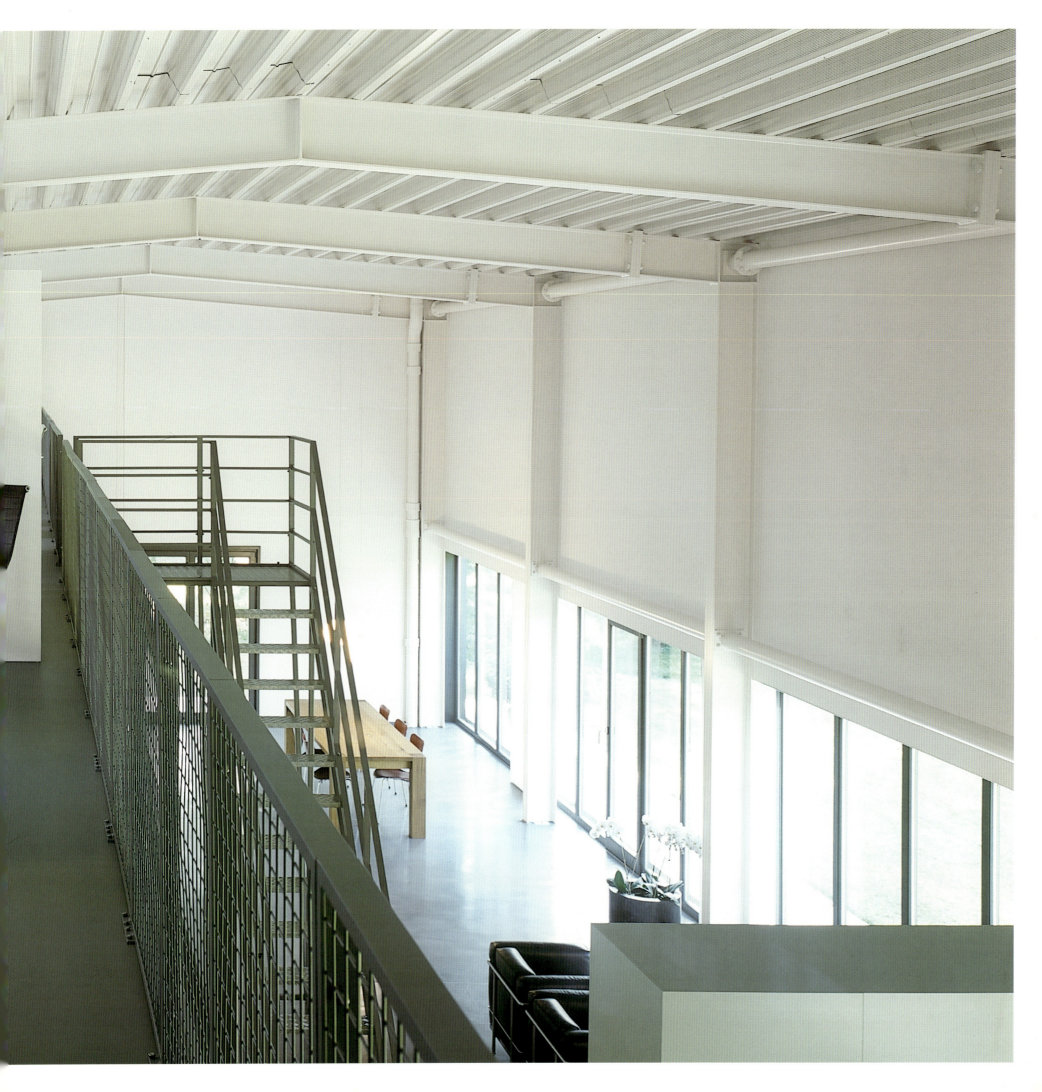

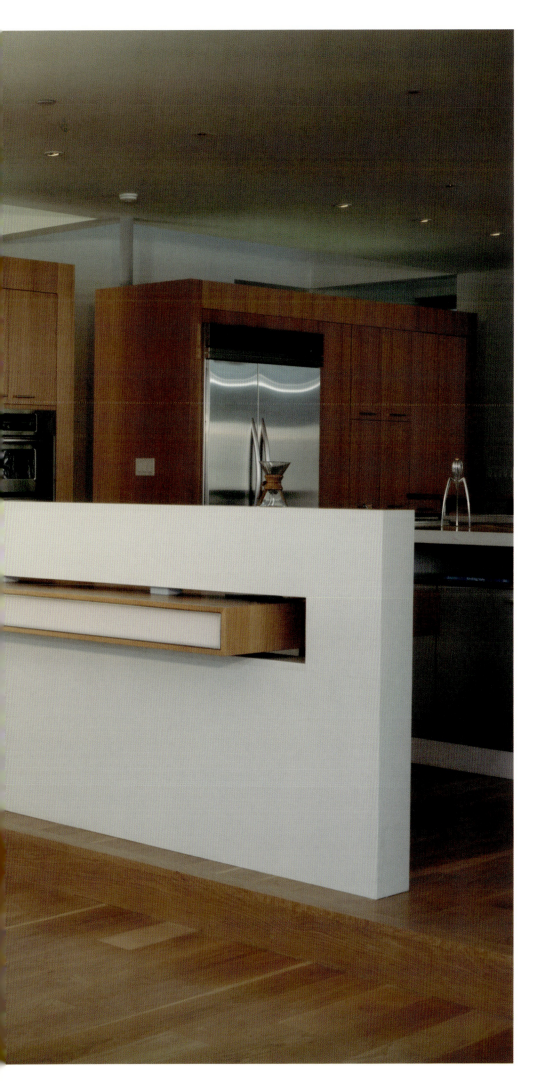

WARTERFRONT HOUSES

HÄUSER AM WASSER

CASAS JUNTO AL AGUA

MAISONS SUR LA CÔTE

CASE SULLA COSTA

Los siguientes proyectos muestran las múltiples posibilidades que ofrece la arquitectura en su relación con la naturaleza, en especial con el agua. En este entorno concreto, en el que deben tenerse en cuenta factores como la posición de la vivienda y su orientación según el sol y los vientos, conviene pensar, sobre todo, en su ubicación con respecto al agua. Ya sea frente al mar o junto a un río o un lago, este elemento natural limita la construcción de la residencia unifamiliar, y las características técnicas adquieren también un protagonismo especial. El límite entre tierra y agua da lugar a oscilaciones climáticas que deben solucionarse para conseguir unas condiciones de temperatura y de humedad óptimas. Los grandes ventanales con vistas al mar de algunas viviendas contrastan con las pequeñas ventanas de otros proyectos y muestran así la multiplicidad de soluciones a un mismo problema. Todos estos condicionantes se reflejan en las obras de los arquitectos, que presentan aquí proyectos con diferentes grados de integración en el entorno. Las viviendas son atractivas por su diseño, por sus formas geométricas y por sus líneas y colores, pero también porque se funden con el paisaje. Así pues, la intensidad física del entorno se siente con más fuerza y la naturaleza se convierte en una presencia imponente que, inevitablemente, delimita el trabajo de los arquitectos. A primera vista, muchos de los proyectos son simples y de líneas puras, pero una mirada más atenta nos revela diseños audaces, creativos y muy sofisticados. Se han empleado diferentes tipos de materiales, desde los propios de las zonas en las que se hallan las casas hasta los más innovadores revestimientos de metal o plástico. En muchos casos son segundas residencias, por lo que las viviendas han sido diseñadas teniendo en cuenta el uso menos frecuente que harán de ella los propietarios. Asimismo, los pabellones independientes, los anexos, los grandes espacios que reúnen varias áreas en una y los interiores de líneas sencillas adquieren un gran protagonismo.

Les projets inclus dans ce chapitre montrent les multiples possibilités offertes par l'architecture dans sa relation avec la nature, plus spécialement avec l'eau. Dans ce cadre concret, qui nécessite la prise en compte de facteurs comme la situation de la demeure et son orientation en regard du soleil et des vents, il convient surtout de penser à leur position par rapport à l'eau. Face à la mer, voire sur les rives d'un lac ou d'une rivière, cet élément naturel limite la construction de la résidence familiale. Les caractéristiques techniques revêtent également un rôle tout particulier. La frontière entre la terre et l'eau suscite des oscillations climatiques qui doivent être résolues pour obtenir des conditions de température et d'humidité optimales. Les grands baies avec vue sur la mer de certaines demeures contrastent avec les petites fenêtres d'autres projets et soulignent ainsi la multiplicité des solutions pour une problématique unique. L'ensemble de ces déterminants est reflété par des œuvres d'architectes qui présentent ici des projets s'intégrant à différents degrés dans leur environnement. Les demeures sont séduisantes de par leur design, leurs formes géométriques ainsi que leurs lignes et leurs couleurs mais aussi car elles se mêlent au paysage. De la sorte, l'intensité physique de l'environnement est ressentie avec d'autant plus de force et la nature se convertit en une présence imposante qui – inévitablement – délimite la tâche des architectes. À première vue, beaucoup de projets sont simples, avec des lignes épurées. Mais un regard plus attentif révèle des conceptions audacieuses, créatives et sophistiquées. Différents types de matériaux ont été utilisés, depuis ceux propres à la région de construction de la maison jusqu'à des revêtements métalliques ou plastiques novateurs. Dans nombre de cas, il s'agit de résidences secondaires. Les demeures ont donc été pensées en tenant compte d'un usage moindre par leurs propriétaires. De ce fait, les pavillons indépendants, les annexes, les grands espaces réunissant plusieurs pièces en une seule et les intérieurs aux lignes simples acquièrent une proéminence essentielle.

I progetti di questo capitolo mostrano le numerose possibilità offerte dall'architettura nella sua relazione con la natura, in modo specifico con l'acqua. In quest'ambiente specifico, in cui vanno tenuti presenti fattori come la posizione della casa ed il suo orientamento in funzione del sole e dei venti, bisogna pensare, soprattutto, alla sua ubicazione rispetto all'acqua. Sia davanti al mare o lungo un fiume o lago, quest'elemento naturale limita la costruzione della residenza unifamiliare. Le caratteristiche tecniche rivestono anch'esse un protagonismo speciale. Il limite tra terra ed acqua crea delle oscillazioni climatiche che dovranno essere risolte per ottenere delle condizioni di temperatura e d'umidità ottimali. Le grandi finestre con viste sul mare di alcune case, contrastano con le finestrelle di altri progetti, mostrando in tal modo le molteplici soluzioni di uno stesso problema. Tutti questi condizionamenti si riflettono sulle opere degli architetti, che qui presentano progetti con vari gradi d'integrazione con l'ambiente. Le case sono belle per il loro design, per le loro forme geometriche e per le loro linee e colori, ma anche perché s'inseriscono nel paesaggio. Così, l'intensità fisica dell'ambiente circostante si percepisce con maggior forza e la natura si trasforma in una presenza imponente che, inevitabilmente, delimita il lavoro degli architetti. A prima vista molti dei progetti appaiono semplici e dalle linee pure ma, uno sguardo più attento scopre dei design audaci, creativi e molto sofisticati. I materiali usati sono di vario tipo, da quelli tipici delle zone in cui si trovano le case, sino ai più nuovi ed innovativi rivestimenti in metallo o plastica. In tutti i casi, si tratta di seconde residenze, e dunque case disegnate tenendo conto di un minor uso da parte dei proprietari. Inoltre, i padiglioni indipendenti, le dépendance, i grandi spazi che riuniscono varie aree in una e gli interni dalle linee semplici, acquisiscono gran protagonismo.

The projects in this chapter explore the immense possibilities of architecture in relation with nature, and particularly with water. In this particular setting, where factors such as location and exposure to sun and winds must be assessed carefully, the house's position with respect to the water is crucial. Whether the projected home is to be on the seafront, by the lakeside or on a riverbank, this natural feature checks the construction of single family homes. Technical characteristics also play a decisive role. The climatic variations arising from the proximity of land and water must be accounted for to achieve optimal temperature and humidity conditions. Panoramic windows onto the body of water beyond contrast in some cases with the small-window designs proposed in other projects, offering a wide choice of answers to a single problem. All these conditioning factors are visible in the architectural works presented in this book, projects by architects with different aspirations when it comes to blending their architecture with surrounding features. These homes are appealing for their design, their geometry and their lines and colours, but no less so on behalf of their ability to melt into their environment. In this way, the physical presence of the surroundings is more forcefully felt and nature becomes an inevitably prominent feature guiding architects' work. Many of these projects are, at first glance, misleadingly simple, with extremely pure lines, whereas on closer examination we discover audacious creativity and very sophisticated thought. Different materials are used, ranging from those readily available locally to new and innovative metal or plastic claddings. In many instances, these designs were for second residences, where the fact that owners would make less frequent use of the house was taken into account. Furthermore, free-standing halls, annexes, large central spaces articulating several others into a whole, and simple-plan interior spaces enjoyed great popularity.

Die Häuser, die in diesem Kapitel vorgestellt werden, zeigen die zahlreichen Möglichkeiten, die eine Architektur bietet, die in Beziehung zur Natur und insbesondere zum Wasser steht. In dieser konkreten Umgebung müssen Faktoren wie die Lage des Hauses und seine Orientierung hinsichtlich der Sonne und den Winden berücksichtigt werden, und vor allem muss die Position des Hauses zum Wasser genau analysiert werden. Egal, ob es sich um ein Haus am Meer, einem Fluss oder einem See handelt, dieses Naturelement stellt immer eine Begrenzung für die Errichtung des Hauses dar. Die technischen Eigenschaften sind bei diesen Gebäuden besonders wichtig. Die Grenze zwischen Land und Wasser ist oft starken Klimaschwankungen ausgesetzt, so dass im Haus optimale Temperatur- und Feuchtigkeitsbedingungen gesucht werden müssen. Die großen Fenster mit Blick aufs Meer, die wir in einigen Häusern sehen, stehen im Gegensatz zu den kleinen Fensterchen anderer Häuser. Sie sind Beispiele für die verschiedenen möglichen Lösungen für ein und dieselbe Problematik. All diese bedingenden Faktoren spiegeln sich in den Arbeiten der Architekten wider, die Häuser schufen, die sich in mehr oder weniger starkem Maße in ihre Umgebung einfügen. Die Häuser wirken aufgrund ihrer Gestaltung, ihrer geometrischen Formen, ihrer Linien und Farben oder weil sie sich perfekt in die Landschaft einfügen, sehr ästhetisch. So fühlt man die physische Intensität der Umgebung mit noch mehr Stärke und die Natur gewinnt an Kraft und Allgegenwart, ein Faktor, der unausweichlich die Arbeit der Architekten stark begrenzt. Auf den ersten Blick handelt es sich um schlichte Bauten mit einfachen Linien, aber wenn man genauer hinschaut, entdeckt man gewagte, kreative und sehr anspruchsvolle Lösungen. Es wurden verschiedene Materialarten verwendet, manche davon aus der Region selbst, oder neue innovative Verkleidungen aus Metall und Kunststoff. In vielen Fällen handelt es sich um Ferienhäuser, weshalb sie unter Berücksichtigung der Nutzungshäufigkeit entworfen wurden. Bei vielen dieser Gebäude spielen Pavillons, Anbauten, große, multifunktionelle Bereiche und Innenräume in einfachen Linien eine wichtige Rolle.

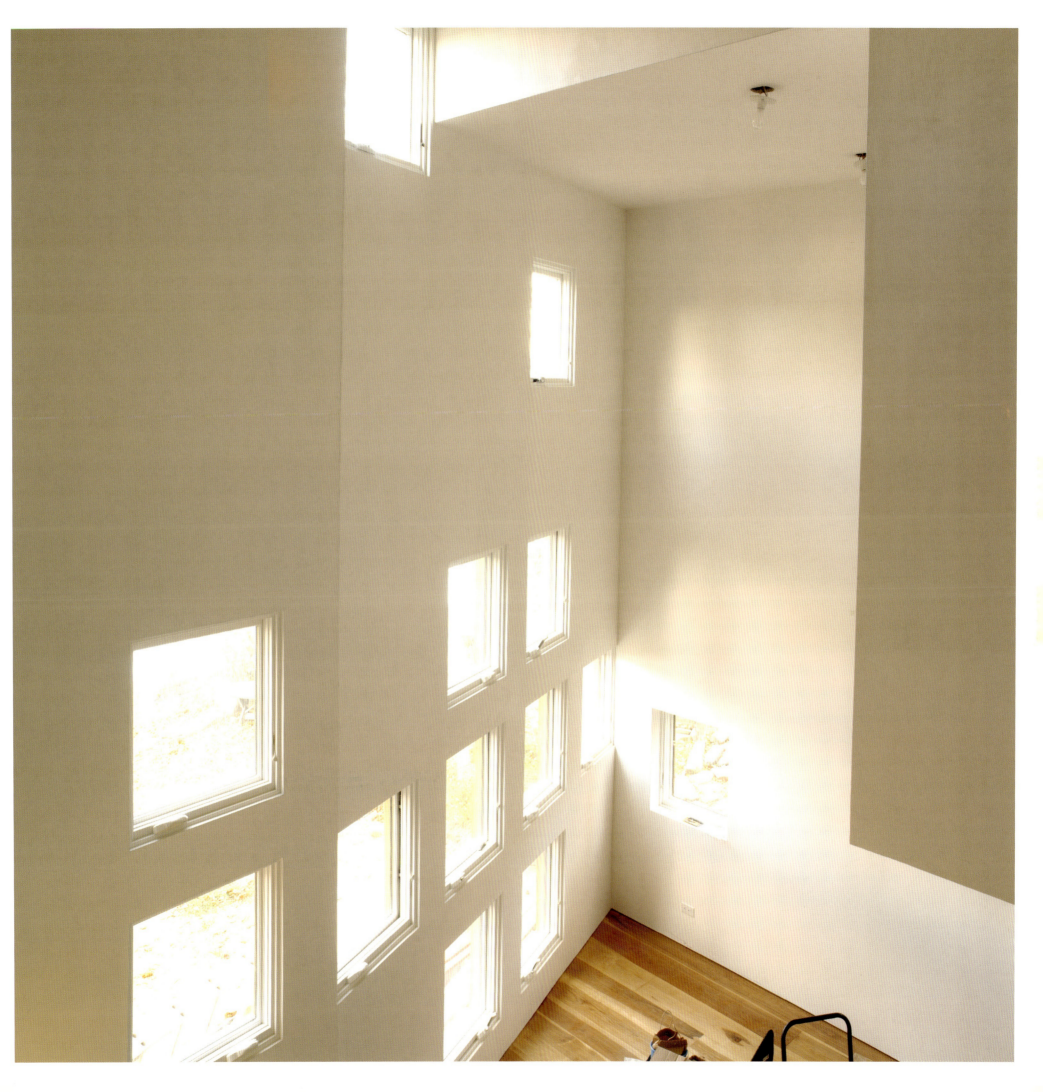

INDEX

A-cero Estudio de Arquitectura y Urbanismo SL
Arriaza 6, bajos
28008 Madrid, Spain
a-cero@a-cero.com
www.a-cero.com
House in Las Encinas | 58
Madrid, Spain
© Juan Rodríguez, Hisao Suzuki

AH3 Architekten ZT GmbH
Hauptplatz 3
3580 Horn, Austria
office@ah3.at
www.ah3.at
House R | 47
Krems, Austria
© Pez Hejduk

Alberto Martínez Carbajal
House in Sitges II | 41
Barcelona, Spain
© Jordi Miralles

Alex Meitlis
2 Vital Street
Tel Aviv 66088, Israel
studio@alexmeitlis.com
House in Tel-Aviv | 10
Tel-Aviv, Israel
© Yael Pincus

Archikubik
Lluís Antúnez 6
08006 Barcelona, Spain
info@archikubik.com
www.archikubik.com
Jacobsen House | 24
Llavaneres, Spain
© Miquel Tres

Architektur Consult ZT GmbH
Körblergasse 100
8010 Graz, Austria
office@archconsult.com
www.archconsult.com
Residence in Graz | 04
Graz, Austria
© Paul Ott

Art' Cittá
Quinta do Assento
4810-811Abaçao, Guimarães, Portugal
gabinete@artcitta.com
www.artcitta.com
Vizela House | 51
Guimarães, Portugal
© Pedro D'Orey

Arturo Frediani
Ctra. de Barcelona 8, entlo.
08840 Viladecans, Spain
akme@coac.net
Residence in Cerdanya | 42
Girona, Spain
© Eugeni Pons

ATT Architekten
Bauerngasse 12
90443 Nürnberg, Germany
att-architekten@t-online.de
www.att-architekten.de
Guggenberger House | 56
Nürnberg, Germany
© Stefan Meyer

BBP Architects
7/25 Argyle St. Fitzroy
3065 Victoria, Australia
info@bbparchitects.com
www.bbparchitects.com
Strathmore Residence | 08
Strathmore, Victoria, Australia
© Christopher Ott

Belzberg Architects
1507 20th Street
90404 Santa Monica, CA, USA
studio@belzbergarchitects.com
www.belzbergarchitects.com
Mataja Residence | 19
Malibu, California, USA
© Tim Street-Porter

Bembé & Dellinger
86926 Greifenberg, Germany
mail@bembe-dellinger.de
www.bembe-dellinger.de
House Caesar | 33
Utting, Germany
© Oliver Heissner

Biselli & Katchborian Arquitetos Associados
Rua Dr. Sodré 117, V. Olimpia
Cep 04535-110, São Paulo, Brazil
bkweb@bkweb.com.br
www.bkweb.com.br
Guaecá House | 64
Guaecá, Brazil
© Nelson Kon

BMD Arquitectos/Tito Dalmau
Passeig Picasso 12
08003 Barcelona, Spain
Casa de las Alas | 07
Barcelona, Spain
© Tito Dalmau

Boncompte i Font Arquitectes/Josep Boncompte
Pau Claris 117, 1º 1ª
08009 Barcelona, Spain
boncompte@coac.net
House in Alt Empordà | 50
Girona, Spain
© Eugeni Pons

Carles Gelpí i Arroyo
Av. Tibidabo 12, 1º
08022 Barcelona, Spain
carles_gelpi@coac.net
House in Puigcerdà | 23
Girona, Spain
© Eugeni Pons

Carlos Ferrater
Balmes 145, bajos
08008 Barcelona, Spain
ferrater@coac.net
www.ferrater.com
Tagomago House | 65
San Carlos, Ibiza, Spain
© Alejo Bagué

Carlos Jiménez Studio
1116 Willard Street
77006 Houston, TX, USA
jimenezstudio@pdg.net
Crowley Residence | 43
Marfa, Texas, USA
© Paul Hester/Hester & Hardaway Photographers

Claesson Koivisto Rune Arkitektkontor AB
Sankt Paulsgatan 25
118 48 Stockholm, Sweden
arkitektkontor@claesson-koivisto-rune.se
www.claesson-koivisto-rune.se
House No. 5 | 20
Nacka, Sweden
© Ake E:son Lindman

Cullen Feng Pty. Ltd.
104/27 Abercrombie Street
2008 Chippendale, New South Wales, Australia
cullenfeng@cullenfeng.com.au
www.cullenfeng.com.au
Silver House | 11
Sydney, Australia
© Eric Sierins/Max Dupain & Associates

D'Arcy Jones Design Inc.
204-175 Broadway East
BC V5T 1W2 Vancouver, Canada
mail@darcyjones.com
www.darcyjones.com
Mosewich House | 21
Kamloops, Canada
© Undine Pröhl

David Luck
7 Hardy Street
3141 South Yarra, Victoria, Australia
david.luck@bigpond.com
www.users.bigpond.com/david.luck
Anglesea House | 66
Victoria, Australia
© Shania Shegedyn

Diego Montero
Ruta 10 y 18 de Julio
Manantiales, Uruguay
info@diegomontero.com
www.diegomontero.com
Forest House | 18
La Barra, Maldonado, Uruguay
© Pedro D'Orey

Edward Suzuki Associates Inc.
Maison Marian 3F, 15-23, 1-chome Seta
Setagaya-ku, Tokyo 158-0095, Japan
esa@edward.net
www.edward.net
Eddi's House | 02
Nara City, Japan
© Daiwa House Kogyo

Elliott & Associates Architects
35 Harrison Avenue
73104 Oklahoma City, OK, USA
design@e-a-a.com
www.e-a-a.com
222 Residence | 46
Oklahoma, USA
© Robert Shimer, Hedrig Blesing

EOK – Eichinger oder Knechtl
Franzjsefskai 29
1010 Vienna, Austria
desk@eok.at
www.eok.at
House on a Lake | 72
Münchendorf, Austria
© Eduard Hueber/Archphoto

FS3 Architekten Felfernig & Strohecker
fs3@untermstrich.com
House Waltl | 09
Styria, Austria
© Paul Ott

Hariri Pontarini Architects
245 Davenport Road, third floor
M5R 1K1 Toronto, Canada
www.hariripontarini.com
House in Toronto | 62
Toronto, Canada
Steven Evans © Hariri Pontarini Architects

Holger Kleine Architekten
Lützowstrasse 102-104
10785 Berlin, Germany
info@holgerkleinearchitekten.de
www.holgerkleinearchitekten.de
Schreibhaus | 30
Steinhuder Meer, Germany
© Werner Huthmacher

Ibarra Rosano Design Architects
2849 East Sylvia Street
85716 Tucson, AZ, USA
mail@ibarrarosano.com
www.ibarrarosano.com
Downing Residence | 49
Tucson, Arizona, USA
© Bill Timmerman

Ice berg
House De Crombrughe | 57
Genval, Belgium
© Laurent Brandajs

Jean-Marie Gillet Architectes
Rue de Verrewinkel 93
1180 Brussels, Belgium
jmg@gilletjm.com
House P | 53
Brussels, Belgium
© Laurent Brandajs

John Friedman Alice Kimm Architects
701 East 3rd Street suite 300
90D13 Los Angeles, CA, USA
jfak@jkak.net
www.jfak.net
Ehrlich Residence | 01
Santa Monica, California, USA
© Benny Chan/Fotoworks

Karla Menten
Romboutsstraat 28
3740 Bilzen, Belgium
info@karlamenten.be
www.karlamenten.be
House D | 28
Hasselt, Belgium
© Laurent Brandajs

Konig Eizenberg Architecture
1454 25th Street
90404 Santa Monica, CA, USA
info@kearch.com
www.kearch.com
Shine Residence | 61
Santa Monica, California, USA
© Benny Chan/Fotoworks

Leddy Maytum Stacy Architects
677 Harrison Street
94107 San Francisco, CA, USA
info@lmsarch.com
www.lmsarch.com
Carmen Residence | 69
Baja California, Mexico
© Undine Pröhl

LIN – Finn Geipel, Giulia Andi
Helmholtzstrasse 2-9
10587 Berlin, Germany
office@lin-a.com
www.lin-a.com
Kleyer House | 54
Oldenburg, Germany
© Werner Huthmacher

Lundberg Design/Ben Frombgen
2620 Third Street
94107 San Francisco, CA, USA
info@lundbergdesign.com
www.lundbergdesign.com
Healdsburg Residence | 44
Healdsburg, California, USA
© Adrian Gregorutti

Lynne Breslin Architects
176 Grand Street 2nd floor
10013 New York, NY, USA
info@lynnebreslinarchitects.com
www.lynnebreslinarchitects.com
Dean Residence | 74
Long Island, New York, USA
© Eduard Hueber/Archphoto

M3 Architects
49 Kingsway Place, Sans Walk
EC1R 0LU London, UK
post@m3architects.com
www.m3architects.com
Highbury Terrace | 06
London, UK
House in Linton Street | 12
London, UK
© M3 Architects

MAP Arquitectos/Marta Cervelló
Teodor Roviralta 39
08022 Barcelona, Spain
map@mateo-maparchitect.com
www.mateo-maparchitect.com
House in Begur | 39
Girona, Spain
© Jordi Miralles

Michael P. Johnson Design Studios
PO Box 4058
85327 Cave Creek, AZ, USA
michael@mpjstudio.com
www.mpjstudio.com
Sullivan Residence | 45
Louisville, New York, USA
© Bill Timmerman

Miquel Adrià, Isaac Broid, Michel Rojkind
Av. Parque de España 3-12
06140 Mexico DF, Mexico
arquine@prodigy.net.mx
F2 House | 52
Mexico DF, Mexico
© Undine Pröhl

MMZ – Marzluf Maschita Zürcher Architekten BDA
Baumweg 45
60316 Frankfurt am Main, Germany
office@mmz-architekten.de
www.mmz-architekten.de
House in Lichtenstein | 40
Dresden, Germany
© Jörgt Hempel Photodesign

Moriko Kira
Nieuwe Batavierstraat 15
1011 LK Amsterdam, Netherlands
info@morikokira.nl
www.morikokira.nl
Weekend House Hakone | 38
Shizuoka, Japan
© Satoshi Asakawa/Zoom Inc.

Nave Arquitetos Associados
Rua General Jardim 808-1001
SP 01223-010 Brazil
navearq@uol.com.br
Schaeffer-Novelli House | 13
São Paulo, Brazil
© Nelson Kon

Pich-Aguilera Arquitectes SL
Àvila 138, 4º 1ª
08018 Barcelona, Spain
info@picharchitects.com
www.picharchitects.com
House in Llavaneres | 25
Barcelona, Spain
House in Tamarit | 37
Tarragona, Spain
© Jordi Miralles

Procter Rihl Architects
63 Cross Street
N1 2BB London, UK
studio@procter-rihl.com
www.procter-rihl.com
Slice House | 15
Porto Alegre, Brazil
© Sue Barr, Marcelo Nunes

Pugh & Scarpa
2525 Michigan Ave, F1
90404 Santa Monica, CA, USA
info@pughscarpa.com
www.pugh-scarpa.com
Solar Umbrella | 14
Venice, California, USA
Orange Grove | 05
Hollywood, California, USA
© Marvin Rand

Querkraft
Mariahilfer Strasse 51
1060 Vienna, Austria
office@querkraft.at
www.querkraft.at
DRA | 60
Vienna, Austria
DOK | 29
Klosterneuburg, Austria
© Hertha Hurnaus

Ramon Esteve Estudio de Arquitectura SL
Jorge Juan 8, 5º 11ª
46004 Valencia, Spain
estudio@ramonesteve.com
www.ramonesteve.com
House in l'Alcúdia de Crespins | 26
Valencia, Spain
© Antonio Jiménez

Rockhill and Associates/Dan Rockhill
1546 E. 350 Road
66050 Lecompton, KS, USA
rockhill@kans.com
Platform House | 48
Missouri, USA
© Dan Rockhill

Satoshi Kuwahara Architectural Studio
211 1-3-5 Daiba Minato-ku
135-0091 Tokyo, Japan
kuwa@kb3.so-net.ne.jp
www.s-kuwahara.com
House in Hakuba | 16
Hakuba, Japan
© Nacása Partners

Satoshi Okada Architects
16-12-302/303 Tomihisa, Shinjuku
162-0067 Tokyo, Japan
mail@okada-archi.com
www.okada-archi.com
Gallery in Kiyosato | 17
Yamanashi, Japan
© Satoshi Okada Architects

SF Jones Architects
4218 Glencoe Avenue
90292 Marina del Rey, CA, USA
mailbox@sfjones.com
www.sfjones.com
Jones Residence | 35
Manhattan Beach, California, USA
© Weldon Brewster

Shaygan Interior Architecture
5 Sebastian Street
EC1V 0HD London, UK
shidehshaygan@btconnect.com
House Fontana | 68
Lugano, Switzerland
© Patrik Engquist

Slade Architecture/James Slade
367 East 10th Street
10009 New York, NY, USA
www.sladearch.com
Pixel House | 34
Heiri, South Corea
© Yong Kwan Kim

SPF Architects
8609 E. Washington Boulevard
90232 Culver City, CA, USA
dafna@spfa.com
www.spfa.com
Brosmith Residence | 59
Beverly Hills, California, USA
Oshry Residence | 22
Bel Air, California, USA
© John Linden

Stelle Architects
48 Foster Avenue
PO Box 3002
11932 Bridgehampton, NY, USA
info@stelleco.com
www.stelleco.com
Berk Rauch Residence | 70
Fire Island, New York, USA
Winner Residence | 32
Long Island, New York, USA
Dune Residence | 71
Long Island, New York, USA
© Jeff Healey

Steven Holl Architects
450 W 31st Street 11th floor
10001 New York, NY, USA
mail@stevenholl.com
www.stevenholl.com
Nail Collector's House | 73
Upstate, New York, USA
© Andy Ryan

SUWA
3B 1-9-19, Yoyogikouen Q-Bldg
Tomigaya, Shibuya-ku
151-0063 Tokyo, Japan
archi@s-uwa.com
www.s-uwa.com
House in Ibaraki | 30
Ibaraki, Japan
© Nacása & Partners

Takao Shiotsuka Atelier
301, Shin-oita 2bld, 4-1-24, Miyakomachi
870-0034 Oita-shi, Oita, Japan
shio-atl@shio-atl.com
www.shio-atl.com
Blue House | 36
Oita, Japan
© Nacása & Partners
Atu House | 03
Fukuoka, Japan
© Kaori Ichikawa
AKI Company | 55
Oita, Japan
© Kaori Ichikawa

Tezuka Architects/Takaharu Tezuka, Yui Tezuka, MIAS/Masahiro Ikeda
1-19-9-3F, Todoroki, Setagayaku
158-0082 Tokyo, Japan
tez@sepia.ocn.ne.jp
www.tezuka-arch.com
Observatory House | 67
Kanagawa, Japan
© Katsuhisa Kida

Toni Esteve
Costa de los Pinos Residence | 63
Mallorca, Spain
© Montse Garriga

Wingårdhs
Kungsgatan 10A
411 19 Goteborg, Sweden
www.wingardhs.se
Astrid House | 27
Kungsbacka, Sweden
Villann | 75
Goteborg, Sweden
© James Silverman